# There We Sat Down

## Talmudic Judaism in the Making

Jacob Neusner

Abingdon Press
Nashville    New York

THERE WE SAT DOWN: TALMUDIC JUDAISM IN THE MAKING

*Copyright © 1972 by Abingdon Press*

*ISBN 0-687-41631-0*

*Library of Congress Catalog Card Number: 78-172812*

SET UP, PRINTED, AND BOUND BY THE
PARTHENON PRESS, AT NASHVILLE,
TENNESSEE, UNITED STATES OF AMERICA

There We Sat Down

For Baruch and Corinne Levine

רעים האהובים

# Contents

PREFACE ............................................... 9

CHRONOLOGY ........................................... 13

MAPS ................................................. 15

LIST OF ABBREVIATIONS ................................. 17

INTRODUCTION: SOCIETY AND SCRIPTURE ..................... 19

I. BABYLONIAN JEWRY ............................... 26
    i.    Babylonia
    ii.   Parthians and Jews
    iii.  Sasanians and Jews
    iv.  Judaism and World History

II. POWER .......................................... 44
    i.    Jewish Powerlessness
    ii.   The Exilarch
    iii.  The Rabbi
    iv.  Messiah vs. Torah
    v.   Conflict of Myths
    vi.  Reconciliation

III. MYTH .............................................. 72

    i.    The Common Myth of the Middle East
    ii.   Moses-Piety: Moses "Our Rabbi"
    iii.  Academy on Earth and in Heaven
    iv.  The Rabbi as a Holy Man
    v.   Torah-Power
    vi.  Study of Torah
    vii.  Rabbinic Theology
    viii. The Rituals of "Being a Rabbi"

IV. FUNCTION ............................................ 98

    i.    Power, Myth, and Function
    ii.   Rabbinical Authority
    iii.  The Rabbi as Government Official
    iv.  Enforcing the Law
    v.   The People and the Torah
    vi.  The Courts
    vii.  From Schoolhouse to Sovereignty
    viii. Conclusion

V. BABYLONIAN JUDAISM IN ITS HISTORICAL SETTING ......... 129

    i.    Rabbi, Magus, Monk
    ii.   The Elite and the Masses
    iii.  One Torah for All Israel
    iv.  The Rabbinate as a Historical Force

APPENDIX: THE TALMUD ................................. 141

SUGGESTIONS FOR FURTHER READING ....................... 145

GLOSSARY ............................................. 147

INDEXES ............................................. 151

# Preface

In my *History of the Jews in Babylonia,* I give a detailed account and interpretation of what is known about Babylonian Jewry under Parthian and Sasanian rule, that is, during the period in which the Babylonian Talmud took shape, from *ca.* 100 B.C. to *ca.* A.D. 640. The Babylonian Talmud served as the authority for normative practice and belief in Judaism nearly everywhere from the time of its formation to the modern age. The Talmud today continues to govern the life of traditional Jewry, orthodox and conservative, throughout the world, and to provide important guidance for reform Jews as well. So the period studied in my *History* is the seedtime of Judaism.

Here I offer for students of the history of Judaism and of the history of religions in late antiquity a brief recapitulation of those findings of the longer work which seem to me important for the study of religions. While the *History* was meant to treat every sort of problem illuminated by all available evidence, here I focus upon only one issue. That is, What was the character of Judaism in the age in which the classic Judaic tradition took shape and in the place in which the holy book of that tradition was formed?

My description is not theological. No effort is made to treat, let alone to systematize and evaluate, religious beliefs, apart from their role in the religious and mythic life of Jewish society as a whole. Nor is it narrowly sociological, let alone historical, for the data of political and social history are interesting for our present work only

9

so far as they tell us something about religious life. The chrono-
logical form of presentation for that purpose is useless. What came
first and what happened then are not central in the study of the
shape of a religious tradition. The real problem is how to describe
and understand the dynamics of such a tradition. In the case of
Babylonian Judaism, the issue is, How did a few men impose their
vision and their will on a very old religious community, and so
reshape that community to conform to a new interpretation of all
that had gone before? For this purpose, religious institutions and
ideas are more interesting than political and social history. Most
pertinent to our inquiry is the evidence of social and religious change
revealed by the community under study. That change is significant
for the long history of Judaism and may illumine other religious
traditions.

Since this work depends upon already published materials, I have
not supplied it with footnotes or bibliography; these are readily
available in the *History*.[1]

While at Dartmouth College, from 1964 to 1968, I was privileged
to know as colleagues Professors Hans H. Penner and Jonathan Z.
Smith (now at the University of Chicago). While they bear no responsibility for the present work, it was in discussions with them,
particularly in response to questions they raised about the pertinence
of my studies to the study of religion, that the interests of the present
work were shaped. If, therefore, students of the history of religions

---

[1] *A History of the Jews in Babylonia* (Leiden: E. J. Brill, 1965-1970)
    I. *The Parthian Period* (1st ed., 1965; 2nd ed., revised, 1970)
    II. *The Early Sasanian Period* (1966)
    III. *From Shapur I to Shapur II* (1968)
    IV. *The Age of Shapur II* (1969)
    V. *Later Sasanian Times* (1970)
A supplement to the foregoing is *Aphrahat and Judaism: The Christian-Jewish
Argument in Fourth-Century Iran* (Leiden: E. J. Brill, 1970). Also pertinent to
the subject under discussion are *A Life of Yohanan b. Zakkai* (E. J. Brill; 1st ed.,
1962; 2nd ed., completely revised, 1970); and *The Rabbinic Traditions about
the Pharisees before 70* (E. J. Brill; three volumes, in press for 1971-72).
Documentation for the present work will be found as follows:
    *Babylonian Jewry:* $I^2$, pp. 1-22, 178-83; II, pp. 1-91; III, pp. 1-40; IV, pp.
        1-72; V, pp. 1-132.
    *Power:* $I^2$, pp. 53-61, 103-22; II, pp. 92-125; III, pp. 41-94; IV, pp. 73-124;
        V, pp. 45-60, 95-105, 124-27, 248-59.
    *Myth:* $I^2$, pp. 122-56; II, pp. 126-240; III, pp. 95-194; IV, pp. 279-402; V,
        pp. 133-243.
    *Function:* $I^2$, pp. 156-77; II, pp. 251-87; III, pp. 195-338; IV, pp. 125-278; V,
        pp. 244-342.

here find relevant materials, it is primarily because of the constructive questions of my colleagues and the ways in which they helped me understand and answer them.

Brown University has supported, and continues to support, my research, through summer research stipends, paying the formidable cost of typing manuscripts, preparing indexes, and, at present, through a sabbatical leave. No generation of scholars has enjoyed the exceptional material benefits of ours. One needs to try to prove worthy of such opportunities. I am, in addition, indebted to the American Council of Learned Societies for still another research fellowship, in 1970-71.

My teacher Morton Smith extensively criticized the *History* throughout its formulation and composition, then proceeded to supply stylistic and substantive comments to each page of the published versions, on which much of the present work is based. Whatever is accurate and not entirely graceless in what follows is owing to his help. Whatever is not remains the reader's burden, and mine.

The publisher of the *History*, E. J. Brill, Leiden, Holland, graciously encouraged me to proceed with a summary and condensation of parts of the larger work. Dr. F. C. Wieder, director of the firm, shared my view that a brief account of some aspects of the whole should be made more readily available to a larger number of students, particularly in America, than would be likely to read the detailed and comprehensive version.

My students David Goodblatt and William Scott Green read the manuscript and helped with proofreading. I owe them much. The indexes were prepared by Mr. Arthur Woodman, Canaan, New Hampshire, on a grant from Brown University.

Baruch A. Levine, teacher, colleague, and beloved friend, shared in the *History*, both directly and indirectly, from its inception to its conclusion. This work is offered as a tribute to him and his dear wife on the occasion of the second anniversary of their wedding.

JACOB NEUSNER

Providence, Rhode Island

11 Nisan 5731

6 April 1971

# Chronology

| | |
|---|---|
| 586 B.C. | - Destruction of first Temple. Exile of Jews to Babylonia. |
| 537 B.C. | - Cyrus, Persian emperor, permits Jews to return to Palestine, and some go and reestablish Jewish settlement there. |
| ca. 320 B.C. | - The Seleucid heirs of Alexander the Great establish rule over Babylonia. |
| ca. 240 B.C. | - Rise of Parthians. |
| ca. 140 B.C. | - Parthians take Babylonia from Seleucids. |
| ca. 40 B.C. | - Parthians conquer Jerusalem, depose Herod. |
| ca. A.D. 20-36 | - Jewish brothers, Anilai and Asinai, establish barony in central Babylonia. |
| ca. A.D. 40 | - Conversion of Adiabenian royal family to Judaism. |
| ca. A.D. 60-80 | - Establishment of Exilarchate by Parthians. |
| A.D. 66-73 | - First Jewish Revolt against Rome in Palestine. |
| A.D. 70 | - Romans establish rabbinical-patriarchal government in Palestine; destruction of Jerusalem Temple. |
| ca. 114-117 | - Trajan invades Parthia, reaches Babylonia. |
| ca. 120 | - Conversion of Adiabenian Jews to Christianity. |
| 132-135 | - Second Jewish Revolt against Rome in Palestine, led by Bar Kokhba. |
| ca. 135 | - Palestinian rabbis flee to Babylonia and Mesopotamia in aftermath of war. |

13

| | |
|---|---|
| *ca.* 140 | - Romans reestablish rabbinical-patriarchal government in Palestine. |
| *ca.* 150 | - Conversion of Edessan Jews to Christianity. |
| *ca.* 200 | - Exilarch's and patriarch's relatives engage in silk trade. |
| *ca.* 226 | - Parthians overthrown by Persians, who establish rule of the Sasanian dynasty. |
| *ca.* 225-250 | - Jewish autonomous government no longer recognized by Sasanians. |
| *ca.* 250 | - Samuel and Persian emperor, Shapur I, agree on future status of Jewish government: the law of the state is law for Jewish courts, and the state will grant the Jews complete autonomy, self-rule, within that limitation. |
| *ca.* 275-280 | - Kartir, Zoroastrian chief-priest, persecutes minority religious communities. |
| *ca.* 300 | - Founding of independent rabbinical academy at Pumbedita. |
| *ca.* 310-330 | - Rabbis claim to be exempt from Iranian taxes. |
| *ca.* 350 | - Exilarch establishes firm control over rabbinical movement. |
| *ca.* 340-410 | - Severe persecution of Christianity. |
| *ca.* 450-470 | - Persecution of Judaism and Christianity. |
| 467-468 | - Jews of the Persian city of Isfahan, expecting Messiah, attack local Magi. Jewish schools closed, synagogues suppressed, rabbis and exilarch killed. |
| *ca.* 500 | - Restoration of Jewish autonomy. |
| *ca.* 450-650 | - Formation of Babylonian Talmud. |

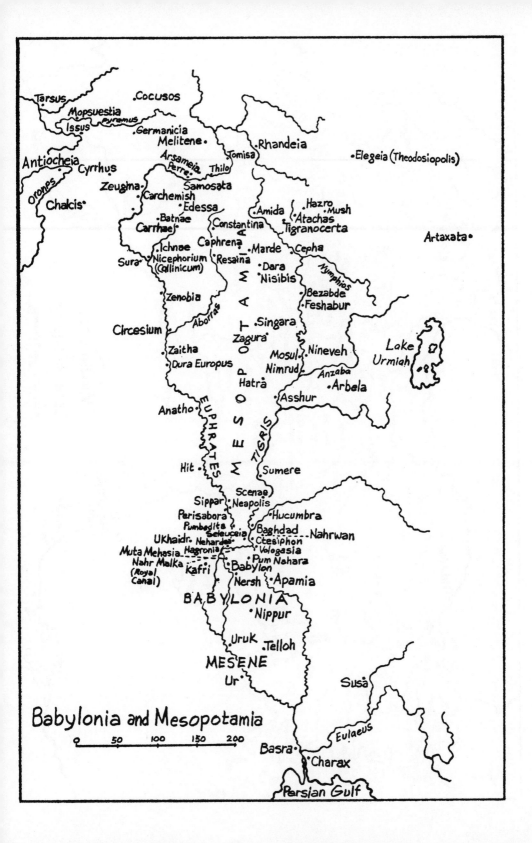

Babylonia and Mesopotamia

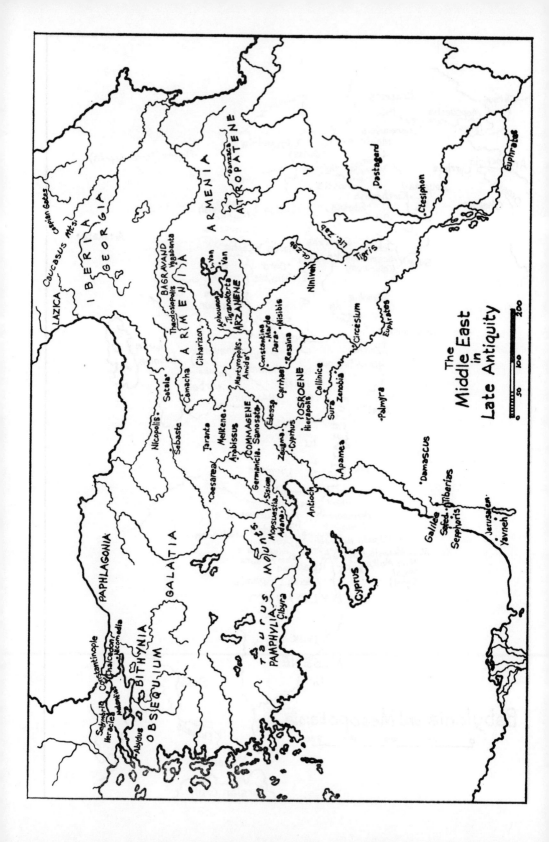

The
Middle East
in
Late Antiquity

0  50  100  200

# List of Abbreviations

| | | | | |
|---|---|---|---|---|
| A.Z. | = 'Avodah Zarah | | Lev. | = Leviticus |
| b. | = Babylonian Tal-mud, Bavli | | Meg. | = Megillah |
| | | | Men. | = Menaḥot |
| B.B. | = Bava Batra | | M. Q. | = Mo'ed Qatan |
| Ber. | = Berakhot | | Ned. | = Nedarim |
| B. M. | = Bava Meṣi'a' | | Prov. | = Proverbs |
| B. Q. | = Bava Qamma | | Ps. | = Psalms |
| Chron. | = Chronicles | | Qid. | = Qiddushin |
| Deut. | = Deuteronomy | | R. | = Rabbi |
| Eruv. | = 'Eruvin | | R. H. | = Rosh Hashanah |
| Ex. | = Exodus | | Sanh. | = Sanhedrin |
| Ezek. | = Ezekiel | | Shab. | = Shabbat |
| Gen. | = Genesis | | Soṭ. | = Soṭah |
| Giṭ. | = Giṭṭin | | Suk. | = Sukkah |
| Hor. | = Horayot | | Ta. | = Ta'anit |
| Ḥul. | = Ḥullin | | y. | = Palestinian Tal-mud, Yerushalmi |
| Jer. | = Jeremiah | | | |
| Ket. | = Ketuvot | | Yev. | = Yevamot |

The Mishnah, Babylonian Talmud, and Palestinian Talmud are divided according to tractates dealing with various legal themes, e.g. Berakhot, blessings; Nedarim, vows; and the like. A reference to b. Meg. 11a is to the Babylonian Talmud, tractate Megillah, folio 11, obverse side of the folio.

Used in this book is *The Babylonian Talmud,* translated under the editorship of Isidore Epstein (London: Soncino Press, 1935-1948).

# Introduction:
# Society and Scripture

When the Babylonian Empire conquered Jerusalem in 586 B.C., Judaean Jews were deported to Babylonia, the land between the Tigris and Euphrates rivers near present-day Baghdad, capital of Iraq. There they settled. Psalm 137 conveys the mood of the exiles from Jerusalem and from Mount Zion, where the Temple had stood:

> By the waters of Babylon, there we sat down, and we wept when we remembered Zion.
> On the willows there we hung up our lyres.
> For there our captors required of us songs,
> And our tormentors, mirth, saying,
> "Sing us one of the songs of Zion!"
> How shall we sing the Lord's song in a foreign land?
> If I forget you, O Jerusalem, let my right hand wither!
> Let my tongue cleave to the roof of my mouth,
> if I do not remember you,
> if I do not set Jerusalem above my highest joy!

While the exiles mourned for the destroyed Temple on Mount Zion and vowed to preserve the memory of Jerusalem, they nonetheless set out and built a community that endured for nearly twenty-five centuries, from 586 B.C. to A.D. 1948. Then the State of Israel received the Jews of Iraq in their return to Zion. For the intervening millenia, a Jewish community flourished on the banks of the Tigris and Euphrates rivers and along the canals in between. This volume

19

focuses upon seven centuries of that history—from approximately 100 B.C. to approximately A.D. 640—and in particular upon the religious history of that period.

A historian of the Middle East would not limit himself to that relatively brief period, much less to such an unimportant group of people. A student of the languages of the region would likewise approach with a far wider range of interests. Why is it that for historians of religions, the particular period and people under study are of special concern? It shall be seen that in this period, a number of abiding issues in the study of the history of religions came to the fore in the life of Babylonian Jewry. Furthermore, the particular events and institutions here examined produced a lasting effect upon the history of Judaism from that time to the present.

Both Judaism and Christianity claim to be the heirs and product of the Hebrew Scriptures—*Tanakh* to the Jews, Old Testament to the Christians. Yet both great religious traditions derive not solely or directly from the authority and teachings of those Scriptures, but rather from the ways in which that authority has been mediated, and those teachings interpreted, through other holy books. The New Testament is the prism through which the light of the Old comes to Christianity; the Babylonian Talmud is the star that guides Jews to the revelation of Sinai, the Torah. The claim of these two great Western religious traditions, in all their rich variety, is for the veracity not merely of Scriptures, but also of Scriptures as interpreted by the New Testament or the Babylonian Talmud.

The Hebrew Scriptures produced the two interrelated, yet quite separate groups of religious societies that formed Judaism and Christianity. Developed along lines established during late antiquity, these societies in modern times come near to each other in the West. Here they live not merely side by side, but together. However, while most people are familiar with the story of the development of Christianity, few are fully aware that Judaism constitutes a separate and distinctive religious tradition. The differences are not limited to negations of Christian beliefs—"Jews do not believe in this or that" —but also extend to profound affirmations of Judaic ones. To understand the Judaic dissent, one must comprehend the Judaic affirmation in its own terms.

What is it that historical Judaism sought to build? What are its primary emphases, its evocative symbols? What lies at the heart of the human situation, as constructed and imagined by classical Juda-

20

ism? The answers come first of all from the pages of the Babylonian Talmud and related literature. From late antiquity onward, the Talmud supplied the proof texts, constructed the society, shaped the values, occupied the mind, and formed the soul of Judaism. For all the human concerns brought by Christians to the figure of Christ, the Jews looked to Torah. Torah means revelation: first, the five books of Moses; later, the whole Hebrew Scriptures; still later, the Oral and Written Revelation of Sinai, embodied in the Talmud. Finally it comes to stand for, to symbolize, what in modern language is called "Judaism": the whole body of belief, doctrine, practice, patterns of piety and behavior, and moral and intellectual commitments that constitute the Judaic version of reality.

However, while the Christ-event stands at the beginning of the tradition of Christianity, the Babylonian Talmud comes at the end of the formation of the Judaism contained in it. It is the written record of the constitution of the life of Israel, the Jewish people, long after the principles and guidelines of that constitution had been worked out and effected in everyday life. Moreover, the early years of Christianity were dominated first by the figure of the Master, then his disciples and their followers bringing the gospel to the nations; the formative years of rabbinic Judaism saw a small group of men who were not dominated by a single leader but who effected an equally far-reaching revolution in the life of the Jewish nation.

At the outset the two groups, the apostles and the rabbis, competed for the loyalty of Jews. Wherever, for example, rabbis founded centers for the study of Torah in northern Mesopotamia, there the Christian apostles were shut out from the Jewish community for a period of a century or more. The consequent Christianity in those towns followed Helleno-Semitic lines, and was not formed by people who were originally Jewish and became Christian Jews, as in the case of Palestine. On the other hand, wherever Christian apostles reached the Jewish community before rabbinical circles attained influence, there Christianity took root very early. Local Christian Jews built a churchly community and drew to it gentile converts as well. The consequent configuration of Christianity followed more closely the lines of the Palestinian church, which had similar foundations. Both the apostles and the rabbis reshaped the antecedent religion of Israel, and both claimed to be Israel.

That pre-Christian, pre-rabbinic religion of Israel, for all its

21

variety, exhibited common traits: belief in one God, reverence for and obedience to the revelation contained in the Hebrew Scriptures, veneration of the Temple in Jerusalem (while it stood), and expectation of the coming of a Messiah to restore all the Jews to Palestine and to bring to a close the anguish of history. The Christian Jews concentrated on the last point, proclaiming that the Messiah had come in Jesus; the rabbinic Jews focused on the second, teaching that only through the full realization of the imperatives of the Hebrew Scriptures, Torah, as interpreted and applied by the rabbis, would the people merit the coming of the Messiah. The rabbis, moreover, claimed alone to possess the whole Torah of Moses. This is central to their doctrine: Moses had revealed not only the message now written down in his books, but also an oral Torah, which was formulated and transmitted to his successors, and they to theirs, through Joshua, the prophets, the sages, scribes, and other holy men, and finally to the rabbis of the day. For the Christian, therefore, the issue of the Messiah predominated; for the rabbinic Jew, the issue of Torah; and for both, the question of salvation was crucial.

What draws the attention of the historian of religions to Babylonian Judaism in Talmudic times? The answer is that certain issues of special interest to historians of religions find in the period under study a measure of illumination: first, the holy man, or religious virtuoso, and his relationship to the masses; second, the place of myth in religious life; third, the way in which religious ideas produce social change. In our case, the holy man was the rabbi. The masses were those ordinary Jews who worshiped one God, believed in the truth of the revelation of Moses, and awaited the Messiah. The myth was the Torah-myth both taught and embodied by the rabbi. The social changes we shall follow led to the transformation of masses of ordinary Jews into a community living by the "whole Torah" taught by the rabbis. They constituted changes in the inherited pattern of religious action and belief, surely one of the least tractable cultural forms. The key words that will be used in this study of Babylonian Judaism are *power, myth,* and *function.*

*Power* here means the way by which one man caused another to do his will: How were social patterns effected and maintained? What institutions embodied power over a long period of time, so that the ability of one man to cause another to do his will was translated into the capacity of any man of appropriate status to do the same?

That capacity by definition is external to any particular individual. To be meaningful, power must be routinized, made independent of personality or the random application of force, so that it does not depend upon a particular circumstance or upon a single concrete instance. For example, as long as power comes from the mouth of a gun, it intimidates only those who believe the gun will be fired and fear death, and it serves only those willing to pull the trigger. But for an old, enduring society, that sort of power is virtually useless. It is the power merely to destroy, serving only episodically and effecting no continuing policies or programs.

Society by definition is continuous, the relationships that embody society are both normative and routine, and the structure of society is permanent, for otherwise, there can be no society at all. So, too, power must be embodied in lasting institutions, must consistently affect what people do and how they relate to one another, and must take form in orderly and abiding patterns. An institution standing within such an organization or structure of power cannot depend upon unusual events, such as the advent of a particularly strong personality. Thus a circle formed by a master and his disciples may exhibit a continuing pattern of religious and social relationships, but it cannot be called an effective institution in its own place and time if, when the master dies, the disciples cease to form a group and coalesce into other groups. On the other hand, a school not dependent upon the fortunes of a particular man or circle within its group constitutes an institution and may permanently and continuously affect the shape of the society in which it is located. Our interest in power within the religious life therefore focuses attention upon institutions and movements and their religious bases.

Central to the investigation of power is an interest in *myth:* namely, the stories people told and the beliefs they held to account for and justify the power-relationships they experienced. *Why* did people do what they did? What were the beliefs that men referred to in order to shape, understand, and explain reality? What were the fundamental convictions about reality that underlay all their actions? How did they justify themselves to other men and before God?

The third key word, *function,* means simply how things worked. Granted the existence of power, the ability of some men to coerce others to say and do their will, either by force or, more amiably, by moving them through an internalization of values; and granted knowledge of the imagination of those men and their community, knowledge of their mythic life—granted these two, how did the system work? What was adaptive behavior within such a power-structure? What sort of *history* took place? What institutions embodied the power and the myth, what programs carried them forward, what was their thrust and dynamism? What were the events that at specific times and places realized these abstract forces of power and of myth in historical facts?

These are issues both pertinent to the study of the history of religions and formative of the later history of Judaism, which are illumined by the historical records of Babylonian Jewry. Obviously they do not exhaust all questions to be answered from those records. But they do stand at the top of the agenda for students of religion, and, moreover, predominate, through a multitude of detail, in the Babylonian Talmud, which is essentially a compilation of religiously grounded law.

What form would Western civilization have taken had the Judaic, rather than the Christian, formulation of the heritage of Hebrew Scriptures come to predominate? What sort of society would have emerged? How would men have regulated their affairs? What would have been the shape of the prevailing value systems?

Behind the immense varieties of Christian life and Christian and post-Christian society stand the evocative teachings and theological and moral convictions assigned by Christian belief to the figure of Christ. To be a Christian meant, and means, to seek to be like him, in one of the many ways in which Christians envisaged him.

To be a Jew may similarly be reduced to the single, pervasive symbol of Judaism: Torah. To be a Jew meant to live the life of Torah, in one of the many ways in which the masters of Torah taught.

We know what the figure of Christ has meant to the art, music, and literature of the West; the church to its politics, history, and piety; Christian faith to its values and ideals. It is much harder to say what Torah would have meant to creative arts, the course of relations among nations and men, the hopes and aspirations of ordinary folk. For between Christ, universally known and triumphant, and Torah, the spiritual treasure of a tiny, harassed, abused people, seldom fully known and never victorious, stands the abyss: mastery of the world on the one side, the sacrifice of the world on the other. Perhaps the difference comes at the very start when the

24

Christians, despite horrendous suffering, determined to conquer and save the world and to create the new Israel, while the rabbis, unmolested and unimpeded, set forth to transform and regenerate the old Israel. For the former, the arena of salvation was all mankind, the actor was a single man. For the latter, the course of salvation began with Israel, and the stage was that singular but paradigmatic society, the Jewish people.

To save the world the apostle had to suffer in and for it, appear before magistrates, subvert empires. To redeem the Jewish people the rabbi had to enter into, share, and reshape the life of the community, deliberately to eschew the politics of nations and patiently to submit to empires. The vision of the apostle extended to all nations and peoples. Immediate suffering therefore was the welcome penalty to be paid for eventual, universal dominion. The rabbi's eye looked upon Israel, and, in his love for Jews, he sought not to achieve domination or to risk martyrdom, but rather to labor for social and spiritual transformation which was to be accomplished through the complete union of his life with that of the community. The one was prophet to the nations, the other, priest to the people. No wonder then that the apostle earned the crown of martyrdom, but prevailed in history; while the rabbi received martyrdom, when it came, only as one of and wholly within the people. He gave up the world and its conversion in favor of the people and their regeneration. In the end the people hoped that through their regeneration, if need be through their suffering, the world also would be redeemed. But the people would be the instrument, not the craftsman, of redemption. As we come to Babylonia, we approach the community that came fully to replicate, then to transmit, the values and hope of the rabbi, and that marked the beginning of the realization of Torah in human society.

# Chapter One

---◆---

# Babylonian Jewry

### i. Babylonia

Babylonia, the region of the Tigris-Euphrates valley occupying the rich flatlands around present-day Baghdad, was one of the most prosperous parts of the ancient Middle East. Under the Iranian dynasty of the Achemenids, which, led by Cyrus, conquered the city of Babylon in *ca.* 540 B.C. and established Iranian rule in Babylonia, the country produced one third of the entire surplus agricultural yield of the vast empire. The key to prosperity was an ample, although unstable, water supply. The turbulent rivers were controlled for agricultural purposes by an elaborate system of canals, sluices, dams, embankments, and dikes, which led the flow of water from the Euphrates on the west to the Tigris on the east. Whenever firm government prevailed, as it did throughout much of the period under study, the system was well maintained and so assured prosperity. Neglect by weak or inefficient government, however, quickly diminished the agricultural yield of the country.

The Jews were brought into the region in the years after 586 B.C. by the Babylonian conquerors of Judea. Living along some of the major canals, they shared in the agricultural prosperity of the region. The masses were primarily farmers and artisans, though there are references to a few traders. In Seleucid times (*ca.* 320-140 B.C.), some Babylonian Jews served in the imperial armies, and as far as is known all were loyal to the Seleucid government. When the Palestinian Maccabees revolted against Seleucid rule and established an independent Jewish state (*ca.* 165-140 B.C.), the Babylonian Jews did nothing to assist them.

The Parthians, an Iranian people from northeast of the Caspian Sea who after A.D. 240 gradually drove Seleucid rule out of the Iranian plateau, finally came to Babylonia in *ca.* 140 B.C., thus serving in the east as one part of a giant pincers (the other part was the Maccabees in the west) to destroy Seleucid rule in the Middle East. The Parthians held the region east of the Euphrates until their dynasty, the Arsacids, was overthrown in A.D. 226 by the Sasanian dynasty at the head of the Persians, who were another Iranian people, originating in the southwestern Iranian province of Persia. The Sasanian dynasty held power until A.D. 640, when the Arab conquest overthrew their state and the Zoroastrian religion, which they had sponsored.

Because of its antiquity and changing fortunes, Babylonia by the first century B.C. was a composite of peoples. The civilizations of the region indeed exhibited both mosaic and palimpsest qualities. An extraordinary variety of peoples, languages, and cultures, both indigenous and imported, flourished side by side, not only in Babylonia itself, but throughout the great Tigris-Euphrates river system. In the long succession of world empires, peoples were shifted from place to place, and new political and cultural forms were superimposed upon antecedent traditions. Like the Balkans, Eastern Europe, or the Northeastern United States, various ethnic groups coexisted, preserving separate cultural traits and societies. For example, the language of the army, politics, and government was chiefly Iranian (Middle Persian, Pahlavi, Parthian); of urban life, commerce, and culture, primarily Greek; and of the massive agricultural population, varieties of Aramaic.

From the perspective of Babylonia, the world was divided into three great cultural regions (omitting any reference to India and China): Greco-Roman to the west of the Euphrates; Iranian to the east of the Tigris; and in the middle the "third world" of the Tigris-Euphrates river system. Composed of Semitic peoples; Armenians in the north; Georgians, Iberians, and others still further north in the Caucasus; and other native peoples to the west—this third world was the arena for both political and cultural competition between Greco-Roman and Iranian civilization. The two great powers, Rome and Iran, repeatedly fought to control its lands and trade, enlisting

27

the support of the subject peoples, who were unnaturally divided by the international frontier, but who were united by their respective languages, cults and religions, and inherited cultures.

Among the ancient peoples with whom Jews shared Babylonian farmlands was the Babylonian-Akkadian cultural group, the oldest and best established. Numerous business documents, almost all dealing with cultic matters, indicate that the ancient temples preserved the old way of life, served the ancestral gods, and continued to collect the offerings of the faithful for the support of the priests. The city of Babylon remained inhabited. Until the first century A.D. temple priests there continued to sacrifice to Bel and Beltis, to pray for the king, and to make astronomical observations. The last inscription in cuneiform writing dates from that same time, and the Chaldean, or Babylonian, astronomical schools attracted Greek students long after the decline of Babylon itself.

The second major group was the Greeks, who had been settled in cities of the region by Alexander the Great and his successors, the Seleucids. They preserved the Greek language and Hellenistic literary, dramatic, artistic, political, and other cultural forms and conventions. Although the Parthians were Iranian, they were deeply influenced by Hellenism. A nomad people without highly developed political and cultural traditions, the Parthians readily appropriated what they found attractive in the culture of peoples they conquered. The Greeks themselves were primarily city-dwellers and controlled international trade. Babylonia stood at the natural confluence of trade routes extending to China on the east and Rome on the west. Hellenists in Babylonia also conducted schools for the preservation of Greek literature and the study of philosophy. Greek metaphysicians, astronomers, naturalists, historians, geographers, and physicians worked there, and such able men were quickly taken into the Parthian bureaucracy.

The third major group—the various Semitic tribes, communities, and clans—spoke the varieties of the Aramaic language, and worshiped gods deriving from the Semitic pantheon. Some towns were predominately Semitic in population, for example, Edessa and Palmyra; others, such as Seleucia, were chiefly Greek; Vologasia, later on also Ctesiphon, in the neighborhood of Seleucia, was mostly Iranian. No large city was primarily Jewish, though some smaller towns and many farming villages were.

For a religious elite to attempt to change the inherited patterns of religious and social life of a large and old community, the necessary condition is that the people enjoy security and stability. Had the Jews of Babylonia faced persistent political or cultural persecution or had they lived under unremitting pressures to give up their existence as a separate group, the possibilities of internal change would have diminished. In their concern for sheer survival, the Jews would have resisted any sort of change. But Babylonian Jews before the second century A.D., when the first rabbis appeared in their midst, looked back upon more than seven centuries of stable and secure life. No one attempted to force them to give up their religious tradition. Granted the limits of the social system within which they lived, they faced no disabilities or even considerable inconveniences because of being Jewish. The tendency of individuals to adopt the ways of other communities presumably produced a measure of tension, but it was balanced, if not outweighed, by movement from without to within the Jewish community. Rabbis took for granted that some gentiles would become Jews. On the whole, therefore, the situation of the community was secure and permanent.

## ii. PARTHIANS AND JEWS

When the Parthians came to Babylonia, it was as inheritors of the crumbling Seleucid empire. On the whole, they did not invest and conquer cities, but entered into mutually satisfactory treaty relationships with the inhabitants. The Greeks, for one, had to come to terms with whoever controlled the trade routes to the east; the Parthians held those routes. The Jews, for another, had no reason to fight for the Seleucids or to oppose the Parthians. So long as no one interfered with their internal life, the Jews could accommodate themselves to whatever imperial regime controlled the country. The Parthians, for their part, were a tolerant military aristocracy, well able to reconcile themselves to existing groups within their new empire.

The Babylonian Jews enjoyed prominence their numbers alone would not have given them. They remained in close touch with their nation across the Euphrates. Straddling the international frontier, they could do much to support a power that favored them on one side or to subvert a power that persecuted them on the other. Furthermore, their strategic position was enhanced by the realities of international politics. As the Maccabees in the west and the Parthians in the east opposed the Seleucids at the center, it became expedient for the Parthians to exploit the contacts of the local Jewish community with their western brethren. Later on, in 40 B.C., the Parthians themselves conquered Jerusalem and for a time deposed the Roman ally, Herod, so they were well aware of the potential usefulness of their Jewish subjects at home. In the second century A.D., when the Romans under successive emperors invaded the Parthian empire and besieged the capital at Seleucia-Ctesiphon, in the heart of Babylonia, Jews throughout the Middle East rose in support of the Parthians. Trajan's invasion of ca. 114-117 was stymied in part by Jewish rebellions in his rear, in northern Mesopotamia, as well as by vast Jewish uprisings in other parts of the Roman orient, in Alexandria, Cyrenaica, Cyprus, and elsewhere in Western Asia, possibly also in Palestine. So the nearly four centuries of Parthian rule of Babylonia marked a period of security for the local Jewry. Never in that period did the Parthian government attempt to extirpate Judaism or to persecute Jews because of their loyalty to the Judaic tradition. Religious persecution simply did not fit into the Parthian scheme for governing their empire.

Information on Babylonian Jewry under Parthian rule is not abundant. We know of a Babylonian Jew, Zamaris (Zimri), who, with his feudal retinue, emigrated to Palestine during Herod's reign. Josephus remarks that Zamaris and his five hundred retainers "could shoot their arrows as they rode on horseback," a reference to the famed Parthian marksmanship. Zamaris represented, therefore, a Babylonian Jewish noble who had mastered the arts of war as practiced by the Parthians, exhibiting considerable equestrian skills acquired through lifelong exercise.

In later time, we hear of Babylonian Jews with Iranian names such as Arda, Arta, and Pyl-y Barish. Arda, Arta would be the equivalent of the Hebrew Barukh, justified or blessed; Pyl-y Barish means elephant rider. These Jews dressed like Parthian nobles, in the tall bashlyk (high hat) characteristic of the nobility, and they enjoyed the usual retinue of horses and mules. They were, moreover, well acquainted with the common law, for they insisted that rabbinical collectors of funds for the Palestinian schools supply them with a quitclaim for a silver cup being transported to Palestine. The Babylonian Jewish nobles held that they bore no further responsibility for the cup. Palestinians reported that these nobles had great power: "If they give an order to arrest you, you are arrested, to kill you—you are killed." It may be inferred, therefore, that among the Jews in Babylonia was an upper class of "assimilated" nobility, familiar with Parthian culture and possessing considerable legal learning, as well as authority in the Jewish community.

About A.D. 40, the royal family of Adiabene, a satrapy lying midway between the Parthian capital at Ctesiphon in Babylonia and Armenia to the north, converted to Judaism. Josephus reports that Helene the queen and Izates her son embraced Judaism. The conversions "miraculously" took place at widely separated points. Izates was in Charax Spasinu (Characene), on the Persian gulf where a local Jewish merchant taught him "Judaism." Another merchant did the same for Helene in Arbela, the Adiabenian capital. Talmudic accounts of the piety and generosity of the two converts, as well as of Izates' brother, King Monobazes II, indicate that the royal family made a good impression on the Palestinian Pharisees. In the war of 66-73, the Adiabenian royal family took an active part, providing the only significant assistance received by the Palestinians from across the Euphrates. It may be that the Adiabenians thought they might win substantial backing in Palestine for a projected Middle Eastern empire, depending as well upon their new brethren in Babylonia. Thus, like Middle Eastern principalities from time immemorial, they may have hoped to exploit the temporary weakness or preoccupation of the two great imperial power centers, Roman and Parthian, to establish a large holding.

Josephus reports that two Jewish brothers, Anilai and Asinai, established a "Jewish state" in Babylonia, which lasted from ca. A.D. 20 to ca. 35. That "state" consisted of a local barony at first established by force and later recognized as legitimate by the hard-pressed Parthian government. The times were unsettled. Several claimants to the throne disputed with one another. Thus the Jewish group, important in the heart of the empire, was given added importance under the leadership of the two brothers. One of the claimants to the throne, Artabanus III, legitimized their rule, saying, according to Josephus, "I commit the country of Babylonia in trust, that it may be preserved free from robbers." Since the Jews were only one of several groups in the region, it may hardly be supposed that Syrians, Hellenes, and Iranians, not to mention the native Babylonians, favored this development. As soon as the Parthian administration could re-establish its authority, it did so.

When in A.D. 66 Palestinian Jewry undertook a massive revolt against Roman rule, Babylonian Jews did little, if anything, to support the war. The Babylonians' chief interest lay in the Temple cult. When the Temple was destroyed in the aftermath of the Romans' conquest of Jerusalem during the summer of A.D. 70, the Romans took preventive action to avoid any possible uprising by Parthian Jews; they hired a Jewish collaborationist, Josephus, to tell their side of the story. His history of the war, addressed specifically to "our brethren across the Euphrates," absolved the Romans both of guilt for the war and of the sacrilege of burning the sacred Temple. Sixty years later, in 132, a second great revolt against Rome broke out. Led by Bar Kokhba, who claimed to be the Messiah and who had the support of important rabbis in Palestine, the war lasted for three years and was followed by severe repressions of Judaism. However, shortly before the Bar Kokhba War, the Romans had achieved a peaceful relationship with the Parthian government; Babylonian Jewry, therefore, once again did nothing to support the Palestinian Messianic struggle.

As has been said earlier, Jews, among others, normally profited from their position on both sides of the contested frontier between Rome and Parthia. The exilarch and patriarch of the Jews of Babylonia and Palestine, respectively, cooperated in the silk trade, one of the chief commodities of international commerce. Silk was imported to Babylonia from the Far East, transshipped for reweaving, according to Roman taste, from the coarse, thick fabric of China to the sheer weave desired in Rome, and then manufactured into garments. The textile factories of Syria and Palestine depended upon a steady supply of silk, and it is known that the sons of the Palestinian patriarch and relatives of the Babylonian exilarch together traded in silks at Tyre. Other important rabbis similarly were involved. Other evidences of Jewish participation in the silk trade are found in Christian Syriac sources. Silk merchants were one of the chief vehicles for the transmission of Pharisaic Judaism and Christianity in the Orient; the earliest Christian apostles to Edessa and elsewhere in the Parthian empire were Jewish silk merchants.

### iii. SASANIANS AND JEWS

The Sasanians, who overthrew the Parthian dynasty (*ca.* A.D. 226), originated in a priestly family in Persia and regarded their rise to power as a sign of the favor of Ohrmazd, the god of light. They therefore not only established the Good Religion of Ohrmazd as the state religion and fostered Zoroastrian rites and beliefs, but at the outset thought they were destined to convert other peoples—including Jews, Christians, Brahmans, Buddhists, and Mandaeans—to the worship of Ohrmazd. Throughout their history, the Sasanians attempted to convert Armenia from Christianity, adopted *ca.* A.D. 300, to Zoroastrianism.

Shapur I (A.D. 242-272) set aside the vigorous proselytizing policy of the early Sasanians as far as Babylonia was concerned and encouraged Mani, a prophet who taught a religion of extreme dualism, to formulate a world religion capable of uniting the disparate religious communities of their empires. Mani's religion, Manichaeism, appealed to Zoroastrians, Christians, and Buddhists, but ignored the Jews. He was put to death in *ca.* A.D. 275 during a Zoroastrian reaction after the death of Shapur I. The high priest, Kartir, then boasted that he had opposed the doctrines of all the "minority" communities, including the Jews. But what his "opposition" consisted of is not spelled out in the pages of the Babylonian Talmud, and this suggests that it could not have been a severe persecution, since the rabbis were hardly reticent about recording such persecutions as they witnessed. It was only toward the end of Sasanian rule that the Jews came upon difficult days.

For most of the four centuries of Sasanian rule, it was not the Jews but the Christians who were consistently persecuted. The Christians, particularly after the conversion of the Roman emperor Constantine in *ca.* A.D. 311, not only favored the fortunes of the Roman (now, Byzantine) foe, but also attempted to convert leading nobility and even Magian priests to Christianity. Just as Constantine's conversion to Christianity had followed close after severe persecutions of the church, so, Iranian Christians hoped, the imperial family of Iran might also accept the faith in the wake of the repression of the church. This would mean very nearly the whole civilized world would have come under the cross. But the Christians' hopes were in vain.

For their part, the Jews from Shapur's time onward were guided by the agreement worked out by a rabbi, Samuel (d. *ca.* 260), with Shapur's government. Samuel ruled that the law of the land was law. This meant specifically that Jews would pay taxes, accept the validity of state documents in their courts, and abide by state regulations on transfer of real estate and related matters. Moreover, Samuel refused to mourn the death of Jews during the Iranian siege of a city in Asia Minor, in one of Shapur's raids westward, and this was taken as a mark of loyalty to the state. For their part, the Sasanians reverted to the Parthian policy of extending to Jewry what amounted to complete self-government. The Jews might not only live under their own religious law, but, like other religious communities in the Iranian empire, would be treated as an autonomous community, governed in all other respects by its own civil law and leaders.

This system of treating organized groups within the empire as autonomous, allowing them to govern their internal affairs, was appropriate in the western satrapies of Iran, above all in Babylonia, which was, as has been said, a composite of many separate ethnic-cultural groups. In the Middle East of that day, law was not separated from religion. Not only matters of cult, but also questions of personal status, inheritance, marriage, divorce, familial legitimacy, crimes, and even commerce within the community itself—nearly all aspects of the life of ordinary folk—were part of and determined by religious tradition. The state had either forcibly to convert all groups to its own religion and law or to treat each as autonomous, and it chose the latter way. Consequently the system of government guaranteeing to all not merely "religious" freedom, but also the right to live under law-systems other than those pertaining to the state and its dominant religious-ethnic group, the Iranian Zoroastrians, proved highly effective. In return for the freedom accorded them to live by their own religion-law, the Jews loyally supported the government in its foreign wars, collected the taxes levied on the community as a group, abided by those government-laws that of necessity applied to everyone—transfer of land-ownership, for example—and generally kept out of the way. The only stories of Iranian "persecution" of Jews are related to points at which some Jews violated these laws. Even the head of Christian church, the *catholicus,* ruled Christendom in much the same way; however, because of the continued subversion of Christians, sometimes even including the *catholicus,* matters worked out less advantageously than they might have.

Had the Iranian government adopted a less benign policy, it is doubtful that the Jewish community could have survived for long. It certainly was within the power of the government to exterminate troublesome groups. Shapur II, for example, wiped out the Arab tribes that had preyed on Babylonia during his minority (*ca.* A.D.

34

309-325). Cities were destroyed in war (e.g., Shapur I razed Dura in *ca.* A.D. 256). The structure of the Christian community was obliterated from *ca.* 345 to *ca.* 410, and the survival of Iranian Christianity during those terrible times could not be taken for granted.

A story drawn from the early years of Sasanian rule illustrates the way matters could have gone:

R. Shila administered lashes to a man who had intercourse with a gentile woman. The man [who had been lashed] went and informed against him [Shila] to the government, saying, "There is a man [the rabbi] among the Jews who executes judgment without the permission of the government."

A messenger was sent to him [Shila]. The messenger said to Shila, when he came, "What is the reason you flogged this man?"

Shila replied, "Because he had intercourse with a she-ass."

The messenger said to him, "Do you have witnesses?"

Shila replied to him, "Yes."

Elijah came and appeared in the form of a man and gave testimony.

The messenger said to Shila, "If so, he [the man who had been lashed] was worthy of being put to death."

Shila replied, "Since we have been exiled from our land, we do not have authority to execute."

The messenger said, "Do with him as you like."

While the messenger was considering the case, R. Shila began to say, "*Yours, O Lord, is the greatness and the power*" (I Chron. 29:11).

"What are you saying?" the messenger asked him.

Shila replied, "What I am saying is this: Blessed is the All-merciful who has made earthly royalty on the model of heavenly royalty, and has invested you with dominion and made you lovers of justice."

The messenger said to him, "Are you so solicitous for the honor of the government?"

The messenger gave Shila a staff and said to him, "You may act as judge."

When the messenger went forth, that man said to Shila, "Does the All-merciful do miracles for liars?"

He replied, "Evil man! Are they not called asses? For it is written, '*Whose flesh is as the flesh of asses*'" (Ezek. 23:20).

Shila noticed that the man was about to inform them that he had called them asses, and said, "This man is a persecutor, and the Torah has said, *If a man comes to kill you, rise and kill him first*" (Ex. 22:1). So he struck him with the staff and killed him.

(b. Ber. 58a)

This story shows that R. Shila did exert considerable authority over Jews early in Sasanian rule. However, the Sasanians supervised the activities of Jewish courts, and the aggrieved party now could complain to higher authority than the Jewish regime, something unknown earlier. That meant, in effect, that the Jewish courts— which were in fact the administrative authorities for Jewry—could not enforce their own laws and act autonomously, but had to subject themselves to state-law.

The real issue was whether the Jewish courts possessed the power autonomously to govern the life and dispose of the property of Jews. If not, they could not be called an effective government. The earliest political response by Jewish authorities to the rise of the Sasanians was inept. Through subterfuge, the officials sought to maintain their earlier freedom of action, keeping the Jews in line by force, while at the same time attempting to deceive the Sasanian bureaucracy. Such a policy, which would have been unnecessary under the lenient Parthians, was impossible under the strict Sasanians, who clearly intended to impose effective control on all their subjects. Their rise to power, unlike that of the Parthians, left them with no good reason to conciliate the Jewish government or that of other groups. The Sasanians believed they owed everything to Ohrmazd, nothing to the collaboration of minority groups.

A more realistic policy for Jewry required formulation. As discussed earlier, this policy came from the rabbi Samuel. He assured the state that the Jews would keep relevant state-law, thus making it unnecessary to oversee the Jewish courts. At the same time the state left it in the hands of the Jews' own authorities to enforce their communal law. It was a fair compromise. But it was possible only after the original enthusiasm of the conquering Zoroastrians had been tempered by knowledge of the ethnic realities of their diverse empire.

iv.  JUDAISM AND WORLD HISTORY

On what basis did Samuel and other authorities of the third century and afterward come to an essentially submissive, quietistic policy toward the imperial government? How could they justify collaboration with a pagan empire? Was it merely a matter of submitting to superior force? If Jews in Palestine and elsewhere in the Roman Empire had rebelled against a government which they regarded as hostile, had wreaked havoc in Alexandria, Cyrenaica, and elsewhere in Trajan's time (not to mention the devastating revolts in Palestine in 66-73 and 132-135), would one not have expected a similarly active and belligerent policy of Babylonian Jewry toward the Sasanians? Jewish authorities in Sasanian times were no less loyal to the Torah than their brethren under Roman rule. How is it, then, that some of them were prepared to compromise and accept the government of a pagan emperor who called himself the king of kings? Why did they not encourage the Jews to fight against the Sasanians rather than to accept the legitimacy of their rule?

The answer lies in the earliest formulation of a policy toward gentile governments, after the destruction of the Temple of Jerusalem in A.D. 70, when the Pharisaic rabbis first came to power in Palestine itself. The two most consequential events in the ancient history not only of the Jews, but also of Judaism, came in A.D. 70 and 226.

In A.D. 70 the destruction of the Temple at Jerusalem confronted the Jews with a disaster of impressive magnitude. They had believed in their own reformation, having learned the lessons of the destruction of the first Temple in 586 B.C. and having applied them in the reconstruction of their state afterward, and that they had achieved reconciliation through the penitential experience of exile. They thus expected that the restored sanctuary of Jerusalem would stand inviolate forever. Indeed, in reflecting on the destruction of 70, they could point only to "causeless hatred" among Jerusalemite society as the reason for the destruction (a valid political perception since the internecine fighting within the walls of the besieged city did make the Romans' task considerably easier).

For Babylonian Jewry, the Sasanians' overthrow of the Parthian regime represented a similarly ominous event. From 597 B.C. to A.D. 226, Babylonian Jewry had never lived under a hostile regime. The Babylonians had given them rich lands; the Persians had sought their support; the Seleucids had used them to pacify revolted regions and, whatever their Palestinian policy, had favored the Babylonian community; and the Parthians had raised them to a position of international prominence, treating them with great deference. The Sasanians, by contrast, destroyed synagogues and drastically altered the Jews' former status.

In A.D. 70, Yoḥanan b. Zakkai, leader of the rabbinical group, founded at Yavneh, a small coastal town in Palestine, an academy

37

for the study and application of Torah to the lives of surviving Jews. While many thought that the Jews' disaster meant they were the rejected children of God, Yoḥanan concentrated on the present needs of the surviving remnant. He devised a program for the reconstruction of the people and the faith in the aftermath of disaster. That program did not include the teaching that by fighting a Messianic war, the Jews would recover their holy city. Instead Yoḥanan taught that just as punishment had surely followed the sin of the people, so would redemption certainly follow repentance. Obeying the will of God prevented nations from conquering Israel; disobeying the will of God subjected Israel to the most abject peoples. And what God wanted from Israel was not a Messianic war but irenic acts of loving-kindness, the atonement for the new age in place of the old Temple sacrifices. Yoḥanan did believe the Messiah would come, and he hoped for divine intervention in history. He did not offer a long-term program of political passivity and religious inwardness merely for the sake of security and social stability; rather he sought a more effective means of continuing to participate, possibly even in the leading role, in the redemptive drama of history.

The advent of the Sasanians in Babylonia produced a parallel spiritual crisis. Believing that the end of days (which must surely come) would be hastened by the advent of the new world empire, the Jews' attention turned once again to the character of the Messianic age, the conditions that would presage its coming, and the time of its arrival. In Palestine during the second and third centuries, the rabbis' definition of the Messianic hope had effected a radical transformation. Instead of offering an activist, military program for subversion of Roman rule, the rabbis' Messianic program now constituted an irenic, spiritualized, passive expectation.

In the new formulation, as evidenced in the sayings of a third-century teacher, Yoḥanan b. Nappaḥa, Roman power was seen as irresistible. Her dominion would continue indefinitely, and those who undertook to oppose her rule prematurely and disastrously would hasten the Messianic redemption in a form no one could really desire.

Samuel now encouraged a quietistic policy for Babylonian Jews, and with good reason. A war against the powerful Sasanian regime could not have been sustained. As a minority group, the Babylonian Jews could not long dominate any substantial territories, nor did they possess natural allies in the region. Moreover, there was no reason in Messianic thought of that time for a diaspora community to rebel against pagan rule. Such an action could have no bearing whatever upon the Messianic process, and neither politics nor religion justified a contrary attitude. The rabbis of Babylonia therefore interpreted temporal disasters in such a way as to bank the fire of Messianic fervor and directed the attention of Israel to prayer and to its own spiritual condition as the means for meriting, and thus hastening, the coming of the Messiah. This attitude had characterized Judaism from the time Yoḥanan b. Zakkai taught that if Israel obeyed the will of its Father in heaven, then no nation or race could rule over them, and that the means of reconciliation in the new age —replacing the destroyed sanctuary and its sacrifices—were prayer, study of Torah, and pursuit of deeds of loving-kindness. By the early third century, these ideas met no significant competition in rabbinic circles.

An example of the spiritualization and ethicization of Messianism is found in the saying of Samuel: "When Israel casts the words of Torah to the ground, the pagan kingdom decrees and succeeds in carrying out its decree" (y. R.H. 3:8). The saying of a later teacher, R. Papa (ca. 300-375) conveys the same spirit: "When the haughty cease to exist in Israel, the Magi shall cease. When the judges cease to exist in Israel, the gezirpati [Persian court-officers] shall cease" (b. Shab. 139a, b. Sanh. 98a). This saying, based on Zephaniah 3:15, transformed an unconditional Messianic promise into a conditional one—if this will happen, then the other shall surely come. Likewise Rav, a contemporary of Samuel, explained that it was the sins of the people that caused them to lose their property to the state, rather than any metaphysical cause. Hence it would be necessary to improve their moral life if they wished to alter their historical condition. In these teachings the natural longing of the people for a better age was diverted from political to moral realities and so divested of subversive potentialities.

In addition, Samuel emphasized that the Messianic time would come only after great suffering, and hence ought not to be too eagerly awaited. At the same time he taught that the only difference between this world and the Messiah's time would be solely in respect to the subjugation to pagan governments. Samuel's saying, based on Deut. 15:11, that the poor shall never cease out of the land, underlined his view that the "golden age" would not be an age of either economic abundance or miraculous healing. In guiding Jewry toward a policy of passive acceptance of Sasanian rule, the drastic revision of Messianic speculation in favor of a wholly non-apocalyptic and ethically oriented formulation certainly served the purpose of Samuel, who seemed to cast doubt upon the desirability and imminence of the great age. But that is only part of the story.

Originally it was assumed that the political passivity of the Babylonian rabbis, like that of Yoḥanan b. Zakkai, represented merely practical wisdom and political realism. Just as Yoḥanan believed that the Palestinian Jews could not overcome Rome, but would succeed only in bringing about the destruction of Jerusalem and its sanctuary (as indeed they did), so the Babylonian rabbis wisely recognized that since the Jews could not do anything meaningful about the Sasanians, they might as well do nothing at all. They were a minority, and had no more valid claim on Babylonia than any other group. The Sasanians were excellent warriors, who, fighting with grand élan, had overcome the hosts of the Parthians and their feudal allies, not once but in three great battles. The Jews could hardly hope to succeed where the Parthians had failed. And they had no very valid reason to try. Hence it was good social policy to keep the people calm, and to avoid calling them to another "holy war" in a futile cause, even though the times seemed propitious.

In spite of the first assumption, however, an examination of the prayers composed by Rav and Samuel reveals extraordinary theurgic activity, which was merely masked by political quietism. It must be kept in mind that the rabbis believed God heard and answered prayer, and therefore for them an act of prayer was in its way just as powerful as an act of violence. Two pertinent texts are noted; one is the abbreviation of the Eighteen Benedictions composed by Samuel, the other, prayers for the New Year and Day of Atonement attributed to Rav:

What is meant by "an abbreviated Eighteen"? . . . Samuel said: Give us discernment, O Lord, to know Thy ways, and circumcize our heart to fear Thee, and forgive us so that we may be redeemed, and keep us far from our sufferings, and fatten us in the pastures of Thy land, and gather our dispersions from the four corners of the earth, and let them who err from Thy commandments be punished, and lift up Thy hand against the wicked, and let the righteous rejoice in the building of Thy city and the establishment of the temple and in the exalting of the horn of David Thy servant and in the preparation of a light for the son of Jesse Thy Messiah;

before we call mayest Thou answer; blessed art Thou, O Lord, who hearkenest to prayer.

(b. Ber. 29a)

To Rav is assigned the following:

This day, on which was the beginning of the works [of creation], is a memorial for the first day, for it is a statute for Israel, a decree of the God of Jacob. Then also sentence is pronounced upon countries, which of them is destined to the sword, and which to peace, which to famine and which to plenty; and each separate creature is visited thereon and recorded for life or for death.

(Leviticus Rabbah 29:1)

Samuel did not set the text of the original prayer, but rather composed a summary of it. In his précis he laid emphasis on the Messianic images of the old liturgy, including the return to Zion, the rebuilding of the Temple, and the coming of the Messiah. Thus Samuel stressed the Messianic and eschatological aspects of the Eighteen Benedictions which were said in public worship three times a day.

Rav's prayer for the New Year reaffirmed that the wonders of creation, being celebrated that day, themselves testified to the enduring sovereignty and concern of Israel's God, who passed sentence on all nations and decided which, in those troubled times, were destined to the sword and which to peace. He stressed the sovereignty of the God of Jacob. So for both the nations and the individual, God's rule was vividly reaffirmed in a time when some might have come to doubt it.

The prayers brought more than reassurance that God continued to reign and knew what was happening. If the people believed that God heard their prayer, then a liturgical composition such as Samuel's would be regarded as powerful not only on earth but in heaven as well. Political quietism, therefore, did not exhaust the rabbis' counsel to Israel. It was through prayer that Jewry should act, and act effectually. Political passivity, even renunciation, did not represent a slavish acceptance of the given nor a submission to the facts of history, but was really a mask for religious, even theurgic, activity.

In so counseling, the rabbis were following the example of Jere-

41

miah, who before the destruction of the first Temple in 586 B.C. had advised the Palestinian Jews to submit to, and the Babylonian Jews not to rebel against, the Babylonians. The exile was decreed as a necessary means of purifying what had been made unclean—the soul of Israel. So he wrote, in chapters 28 and 29, that only false prophets promise good cheer, and that Babylonian Jews should settle down for seventy years. But in chapter 51 (whether it was by Jeremiah or not, the rabbis thought it was), Jeremiah issued fearful curses and dire predictions of the end of Babylonia itself, which he recorded in a book and sent to Babylon to be cast into the Euphrates, with the proclamation, a magical omen, "Thus shall Babylon sink, to rise no more, because of the evil which I am bringing upon her." Jeremiah 51 is the necessary concomitant to Jeremiah 28–29. While in chapters 28–29, Jeremiah told the Babylonian Jews to settle, in chapter 51 he issued curses against Babylonia—curses which, he believed, would produce the destruction of their rule. Thus the Jews should rely upon the intervention of God for redemption from Babylonia.

The rabbis could offer a policy of passivity precisely because they believed they had another, better way of meeting the crisis. In their exegeses they avoided any messages they found inappropriate or inopportune. But this, too, followed the example of Jeremiah, whose public message was to submit and to take heart, but who acted in a manner calculated to enlist supernatural power in the restoration of Israel's prosperity.

Furthermore, Rav, Samuel, and the other rabbis invested their best energies in the legal reformation of Babylonian Jewry, following the lines of the Mishnah, the code of the oral Torah, which had been promulgated by Rabbi Judah, the patriarch in Palestine a generation earlier. They themselves were lawyers and judges, and the bulk of the studies conducted in their academies concerned the law. They used their power to realize in Jewish affairs the teachings of the Torah as they understood it. As a result of rabbinical teaching and judicial activities, Babylonian Jewry came, in succeeding generations, to approximate the high ethical and legal standards of the rabbis. Rabban Yoḥanan b. Zakkai had similarly devoted himself to legal studies and teaching.

The emphasis upon the formation of a just and wholesome society was not new in these later generations. The prophets had taught that the state of society was decisive in forming national history and that the most humble daily affairs must, for the safety and prosperity of the state, be conducted in righteousness and justice. The eschatological significance of law-observance in the minds of the rabbis must not be ignored if the reader is to perceive fully the way in which they responded to the great historical events of the day. Their emphasis on the conditional quality of redemptive promises has already been observed: "If Israel obeys the will of their Father in heaven, then no nation or race can rule over them." "When Israel casts words of Torah to the ground, the heathen are able to decree and carry out their decrees." "When the haughty will cease in Israel, then the gendarmes will cease among the Iranians." These words were not idle homilies; they provide the key to understanding why such stress was laid upon the legal and social reformation of Israel. It was through the realization of the Torah, especially of its social ideals, in the life of Israel that the rabbis intended to bring redemption.

The converse of Samuel's sayings should be considered: "If Israel kept the law, then they would no longer be subjected to the decrees of the pagan nations, who would not be able to decree and carry out their decrees." This statement bore more than political weight, for Samuel also said, "The Messianic age differs from this world only in respect to subjugation to the pagan empires." The converse was that when Israel no longer was subjected to pagan rule, that fact in itself would signify the redemption. If Israel kept the will of their Father in heaven, the decrees of the pagans would be nullified, and for Samuel that very nullification would signify the advent of the time to come.

The achievement of justice and mercy, the protection of the rights of the poor and weak, the establishment of a serene and decent social order according to the Torah's requirements—these were crucially important because through them, as well as through prayer, Israel would carry out its side of the Messianic contract. Prayer, study, and fulfillment of the Torah, therefore, represented a very vigorous response to the cataclysmic events of the age, and from the rabbis' perspective, embodied more powerful instruments than any other for the achievement of the better age for which Jews longed. Prayer, study, deeds—these three, but of greatest historical consequence was the legal and judicial enterprise.

43

# Chapter Two

———◆———

# Power

## i. JEWISH POWERLESSNESS

From the perspective of the Sasanian government at Ctesiphon, the Jews, like other minority communities, did not exercise much power. They fielded no armies, exerted no influence in affairs of state, controlled no appointments in the government bureaucracy, shaped no foreign policies or domestic programs. For example, Jews may, at least for a time, have served as canal inspectors. However, they did not decide whether and where to build canals, nor did they supply the capital needed for construction.

Their prosperity and their very lives depended upon the imperial regime. In times of war they were mere pawns. In A.D. 363 when the Roman emperor Julian invaded Babylonia, his historian, Ammianus Marcellinus, reported that a Jewish town was razed and the inhabitants fled. They were able to return only after Shapur II's brilliant strategy forced the Roman invaders to retreat. But the Jews themselves had done nothing to contribute to shaping or effecting that strategy. The government was able to move populations here and there in its empire. From Armenia, Jews and Christians were deported to Persia; neither group had much say in their removal. However, generally the exalted Sasanian king of kings and his ministers looked benignly on the Jewish group, did what they thought good for them, served as patrons for their welfare, and, on the whole, made a success of it.

The Jews, for their part, looked to "the *King* of the king of kings, the Holy One, blessed be he." As discussed in Chapter One, they sought in their own way to exercise another kind of power, that which derived from heaven. On earth they regarded the trivial affairs of their villages and towns as having supernatural importance. If their activities seemed petty to the great ministers of state, to the people of the villages they did not. This was quite natural. While one may have wanted to share in the decisions on whether Iran should go to war against Rome or whether the state should intensify its investment in the water supply and agriculture of a vast region, he could exercise a say-so concerning only humble matters: food served on the table, conduct in the local marketplace, prayers said in the synagogue, planting crops, raising children, and making marriages. Somewhat paradoxically, these seemingly petty matters were understood by the rabbis and by ordinary Jews as well to be of greater weight in the final determination of world history than the amassing of vast armies and the siege of great cities.

At the head of the Jewish community from the first century onward stood the *exilarch,* the ruler of the Jewish community in exile. He was supported by the Iranian government in power, first the Parthians, later, after an interval, the Sasanians. His authority over the Jews depended upon that support. Normally, Jews could not appeal over his head to the government, and his decisions therefore had the effect of law for Jewry. He certainly wielded the force necessary to carry out his will. He collected the governmental taxes levied upon Jewry as a whole and transmitted them to the court at Ctesiphon. He represented Jewry at court, when needed, and effected government policies among the Jews. At the head of the state stood the all-powerful king of kings, radiating power through various bureaus and departments of government down to the farms and streets of the empire; at the head of the Jewish state-within-the-state stood the exilarch.

The exilarch's government consisted of local bureaus, or courts, which adjudicated disputes, supervised commerce and trade, enforced the law, collected taxes, and did all the other things at the village level for which the exilarch was responsible to the court at Ctesiphon. As will be seen, the staffing of some of these local courts by rabbis was at first an effort to secure better-trained and more effective, disciplined administration. The neat pyramid described above was a fantasy. For several reasons no government could actually work as efficiently as the scheme suggests. First, communication was poor. What was done in a village could not be readily supervised, nor could errors be rapidly rectified. The will of the exilarch might be expressed, but an intervening, second-level bureaucracy which would oversee the work of the local courts was rarely available. Local prejudice, custom, and vested interests thwarted the ready realization of the exilarch's—or the emperor's—wishes. Second, regardless of the authority at the disposal of the exilarch, he would have required a considerable police force to oversee and carry out his policies. The Jews did not live in a single, compact territory, but were spread through the canal system of the region. One man could not be everywhere. Even under the best circumstances, government in antiquity was considerably less efficient than it is today.

The power available within the Jewish community may be characterized as derivative, episodic, and inconsequential. It derived from the wishes of men and from forces external to Jewry. Dependent upon local practices, it was effected only when instruments for its realization were present, and these were available not routinely, but only on occasion. And what Jews did, did not make a great deal of difference in the larger world in which Jews found themselves. Therefore, when one speaks of power and of the structure by which power was organized, mediated, and brought to bear, he must use incongruously grand concepts to explain trivialities. That structure, as observed, was loose, fragile, and one-dimensional. It consisted of a power-center—the subordinated exilarch and his little administration—with local authorities standing in a loose relationship to the center, in control of the administrative courts of the villages and towns.

## ii. THE EXILARCH

The exilarchate began to function effectively in the second half of the first century. Whether it actually was older than that—possibly dating back to the time of Jehoiachin at the beginning of the sixth century B.C., as was commonly believed—cannot be said. However, the only concrete information presently available about the politics of first-century A.D. Babylonian Jewry contains no reference to an exilarch, even while discussing important matters in which an exilarch, if there were one, should have been involved.

During the troubled time in the first half of the first century, when one Parthian pretender after another seized the throne, Babylonia, like the rest of the Parthian empire, enjoyed no secure government at all. As noted in Chapter One, two Jewish brothers, Anilai and Asinai, during the confusion seized power in central Babylonia, ruling not only the Jewish communities but the whole area. They set up their own government, which lasted for nearly two decades.

The chaos began to abate with the rise of the Parthian emperor, Vologases I, in the middle of the first century A.D. While the indecisive struggle between Parthia and Rome, ending in about A.D. 65, may have weakened his government, a number of his constructive efforts curbed the power of the Parthian nobles and established a secure frontier with both Rome and Armenia (although Roman preoccupation with Palestine from A.D. 66 to 73 must also be considered as a factor). Vologases I achieved something which had been unknown in Parthia for more than half a century: he held power through several decades, managing to avoid both foreign disasters and internal strife. His foundation of Vologasia, near Seleucia-Ctesiphon, doubtless greatly assisted the expansion of the silk trade with China on the east and with Palmyra and the Mediterranean coast, and this increasingly profitable trade probably provided new financial resources for the throne.

If the story of the Jewish "barony" of Anilai and Asinai in and around Nehardea from ca. A.D. 20 to 36 is historical, then the Parthian central government must have had to give considerable attention to the government of this numerous ethnic minority. The very position of the great areas of Jewish settlement required it, for the Jews formed a large segment of the settled population around the winter capital of Ctesiphon, the Greek city of Seleucia, and the new emporium at Vologasia. The Jewish population surrounding the heart of the empire had to be suitably governed. From the Babylonian Jews' establishment of their own state in ca. A.D. 20-36, it must have been clear to the reforming administration of Vologases that Jews in Babylonia were not adequately controlled.

What choices were open to the Parthian authorities? First, they could, of course, ignore the problem, allowing events to take their natural course in the Jewish territories and settlements. This was manifestly unsatisfactory, for Vologases sought to establish effective government and could not overlook the inevitable chaos that would have resulted from ignoring the behavior of the Jews in Babylonia, where his capital was located. Second, they could attempt to include the government of the Jewish ethnic groups within the territorial sovereignties of other places. The Jews around Seleucia could have been placed under the Greek authorities of that city (as doubtless those in the city itself were). But this course of action would have been unsatisfactory, since the Greek cities at this time were not the regime's most loyal adherents. Furthermore the Jews and the Greeks hated each other; the Greeks had fought Anilai and Asinai. And the Jewish settlements were too extensive for incorporation into surrounding political units; at the same time they were not sufficiently compact or concentrated to form a separate unit.

An ideal solution was to establish among the Jews in Babylonia an ethnic authority of their own, much like that which probably existed after the destruction of the first Temple in Babylonian and in Achemenid times. If such an authority could develop and win the loyalty of the Jewish population to the regime, then the Parthian government would have accomplished several useful purposes. First, it would assure an effective government in the Jewish villages and towns and over Jewish minorities in the Greek and Iranian settlements. Second, it would secure the peace of strategically vital territories near the capital. Third, in time the Parthians might make use of the authority so constituted to advance their own foreign policy through an exploitation of the Jewish authority's connections with Jews in Roman Palestine. There is every evidence that some Jews in Palestine and throughout the upper Mesopotamian valley did act in a manner favorable to Parthian interests at a number of crucial points in the second century. Thus it was in the interest of the Parthian government, both during its period of reorganization under Vologases I and afterwards, either to found or to encourage and support the foundation of a Jewish ethnarch, or exilarch, in Babylonia.

A further factor played a part in Parthian consideration of the Jews' administration. The destruction of the Temple in Jerusalem in A.D. 70 posed a serious problem to the Parthian government. In former times, Babylonian Jewry, like that in other parts of the diaspora, had been loyal to the Temple. Pilgrims went up to Jerusalem, and Temple collections of a half-*sheqel* were gathered regularly in Nehardea in the south and in Nisibis in the north and forwarded in armed caravans to the Temple. The Temple authorities, for their part, sent letters to Babylonia to advise the Jews on the sacred calendar and other religious issues. After the destruction, the authority of the Temple was assumed by the remnants of the Pharisaic party at Yavneh, where, with Roman approval, the powers formerly exercised by the Temple administration became vested in Yoḥanan b. Zakkai. The Parthians enjoyed the services of an excellent intelligence bureau, and they must have known that the Palestinian Jewish authority would no longer be exercised by quasi-independent officials, but would be very closely supervised by the Romans.

If the Parthians had been willing to allow a limited, and on the whole politically neutral, authority to be exerted from the Jerusalem Temple over their subjects, they would never have permitted such authority to be exerted by what they assumed was a Roman functionary. On the contrary, just as the Romans sought to mobilize Jewish support and to use Jewish officials for their own purposes, so too the Parthians exploited the fact that within their hereditary enemy's territories flourished a large religious-ethnic group with strong ties across the Euphrates and a deep sense of grievance against Rome. They continuously tried to foment unrest among minority groups within the Roman Empire. The Romans, for their part, were keenly aware of the danger of leaving substantial ethnic groups to straddle their borders; for this reason they had invaded Britain and attempted to retain Armenia in the preceding century and a half. They were, moreover, deeply concerned about Jewish public opinion in Parthia, and as a public relations effort had hired Josephus to convey their view of war guilt to the Jews across the Euphrates.

The evidence that the exilarchate was actually created at this time is slight; however, it ought not to be ignored. The silence of Josephus on this point is made very striking indeed by his testimony about how Jews actually were governed by Anilai and Asinai at this time. If there was an exilarch between A.D. 20 and 40, there is no evidence that he was of any import. He certainly did not exert any authority or affect events in any observable way. Evidence that an exilarchic line was founded after A.D. 70 appears in the list of exilarchs given in the *Seder 'Olam Zuta* (Small History of the World). Among those people listed from the time of the first destruction of Jerusalem to A.D. 70, the *Seder 'Olam Zuta* preserves no names or traditions worth taking seriously, and one may conclude that its eighth-century author had no reliable information on the subject. However, the listings after 70 include names that *are* attested in other sources. Following is the list of exilarchs from *ca.* 70 to *ca.* 275:

And at this time Shemaiah died. And there arose after him Shekheniah his son, who is the tenth generation of Jehoiachin the King at the time of the destruction of the Second Temple. . . .

Shekheniah died and Hezekiah his son arose. Hezekiah died and was buried in the land of Israel in the valley of Arbella in the east of the city. 'Aqov his son arose. 'Aqov died and Nahum his son arose after him.

There were sages with him, their names being R. Huna and R. Hinena, R. Matennah and R. Hananel. Nahum died. After him arose Yohanan his brother, son of 'Aqov.

His sage was R. Hananel. Yohanan died. After him arose Shefet his son. Shefet died. 'Anan his son arose. When 'Anan died Nathan remained in his mother's womb.

He is Nathan of Ṣuṣita, *Rosh Golah* [exilarch]. Nathan died. After him arose R. Huna his son. Rav [d. *ca.* 250] and Samuel were his sages.

Since Rav and Samuel date from the end of the Parthian period, we may conclude that the above list covers the period from *ca.* A.D. 70 to 226. Some of the names on it, particularly Nahum and Huna, are attested in earlier sources; and the tradition recorded in *Seder 'Olam Zuta* may well imply the beginning of sound information on an exilarch sometime in the latter half of the first century.

The exilarchate in Parthian Babylonia, like the patriarchate in Roman Palestine, was the most convenient means to manage a potentially useful ethnic group's affairs at home and to exploit its connections abroad. It was a way of annulling whatever influence Jewish functionaries of Rome might exert over Babylonian Jewry by providing an alternate, home-born authority, supported and closely supervised by the Parthian government. Both the exilarch and patriarch were backed by imperial troops. Judah, the Palestinian patriarch [*ca.* A.D. 170-210], had a detachment of Goths at his command. The exilarch possessed an armed retinue. Both eventually achieved great spiritual as well as political influence over their respective Jewish communities. Each was created in part because of the destruction of Jerusalem. The patriarchate was a means of governing internal Jewish affairs in which the Romans had no special interest, while at the same time keeping peace in Palestine. The exilarchate had the same function in Babylonia. At the same time

50

both were intended to prevent aliens from influencing Jews under their control; they themselves were to exert malevolent influence across the frontier where possible.

In the second century, the exilarchate developed into a powerful instrument of government, with its agents enjoying the perquisites of the Iranian nobility. It inflicted the death penalty and governed the Jews by its own lights, enforcing its judgment with military force when it chose. If the several Jewish revolts against Rome, which at times were highly propitious from the Parthian viewpoint, were in fact instigated by its agents, and if the support given in the crisis of Trajan's invasion was the result of exilarchic influence, then the Parthians must have judged the exilarch to be a great success indeed. By the end of the second century, the exilarch Huna was regarded with a mixture of respect and apprehension in Palestine, where his claim to Davidic ancestry in the male line (superior to Judah's allegedly in the female line) was recognized. Among the Jews and Parthians alike, the exilarchate played a major political and administrative role.

### iii. THE RABBI

The rabbis were originally a Palestinian group. Babylonian Jews' first contact with them may have antedated the Bar Kokhba War (*ca.* A.D. 132-135) by a century, but the rabbinical movement first established its characteristic institution, the academy, during that war. Refugee sages, fleeing the terrible struggle and its aftermath, settled in Babylonia.

The main point of interest for this study is the exilarch's relationship to the rabbis. In *ca.* A.D. 140 Nathan, son of the Babylonian exilarch, was sent to school under rabbinical auspices, and he later continued his studies in Palestinian schools. Several other Babylonians in the Palestinian schools, including Ḥiyya, his sons, and his nephew Rav, were probably related to the exilarch. The evidence thus points to the existence of a few rabbis from Babylonia, and a few others in Babylonia, in the second century. Generally those rabbis who lived in Babylonia were colleagues or disciples of R. 'Aqiba and R. Ishmael, the leading masters in Yavneh before the Bar Kokhba War. Those who came from Babylonia were exilarchic relatives. When law-teachers came to Babylonia during and after the war, the exilarch must have provided the means for conducting law schools, just as he had sent his son and was to send his relatives later to study in the Palestinian schools.

The settlement of rabbis in Babylonia was encouraged by the exilarch in his effort to secure well-trained officials. What accounts for the pro-rabbinical sentiment of the exilarch? The exilarch must have had to contend with other Jewish authorities, particularly powerful local figures like Arda, Pyl-y Barish, Anilai, and Asinai. These potentially dangerous competitors for the rule of Jewry were seen to be "assimilated" to Parthian culture. Babylonian Jewish officials were "Parthian" in many ways. They were upper-class Jews who possessed wealth and influence, much like the exilarch himself. One good way of circumventing their influence over the ordinary Jews (who would have had much less contact with Parthian politics, court life, and, therefore, general culture) would have been for the exilarch to present himself as the protagonist of the ancient tradition of Moses, against the local Iranized Jewish elite competing with him for power. The exilarch would then have been able to claim that his rule was legitimate, not merely effective. When the people listened to him, they were obeying the Torah of Moses, and he therefore stood for the ancient revelation of Moses at Sinai. The local Jewish strong-men, however, ruled by force of arms, not by the right rules laid down by Moses. So the ordinary Jews would have been given good reason to favor the central authority of the exilarch over the local rulers.

But how to establish such a public image? How better than to associate oneself with the Palestinian rabbis whose prestige had been rising ever since the destruction of the Temple, and who could send disciplined, learned, and charismatic rabbis to serve the exilarch, to help build his administration, and to bolster his claim of descent from David? Allegedly knowledgeable in the Mosaic law, the rabbis were believed to be holy men and were accredited with wonderful powers. Because of their standing in the community, they could lend prestige to the peculiar political claim of the exilarch. Against such holy men, what could local strong-men or powerful upper-class leaders offer? The exilarchate was a relatively new institution. Because of the terrible invasions and unsettled domestic conditions of the second century, the Parthian government, which had created the exilarchate, was unable to provide necessary support. As a result the exilarch had his hands full simply establishing his preeminence over other, older kinds of local Jewish authorities. The Palestinian rabbis, as well as those Babylonians trained by them, provided a ready and inviting aid in setting up an effective and "legitimate" administration.

Thus the rabbis served to enhance the legitimacy of the exilarchate by providing stronger theological foundations for the exilarch's political power and by attesting to the validity of his claim to be descended from David. Their learning, holiness, and magical powers won the assent of ordinary people to their legal and exegetical doctrines. They were useful to the exilarch, for they could give him what he lacked: a means of influencing the masses, and a source of administrative talent and disciplined, reliable local leadership. In return the rabbis were prepared to collaborate with any political leader who would give them power over Jewry to achieve their religious program. Together the rabbis and exilarch might outweigh the competing, centrifugal forces constituted by older, local grandees of various sorts and in various places.

By the turn of the third century, the rabbinical movement in Babylonia included a few local authorities, such as Samuel, and a larger number of trained and authorized Palestinian rabbis. The movement hardly dominated Babylonian Jewish life, and it posed no threat whatever to the exilarch, who made use of rabbis for his own purposes and was probably glad to have more of them. The exilarch provided the chief source of financial support for the rabbinical schools and of employment for their graduates. He was equally eager to accept the credentials of Palestine-trained rabbis, and to authorize Palestinian rabbinical newcomers to serve in his system of courts as lawyers, judges, and communal administrators.

The exilarch, moreover, was particularly anxious to employ men who could apply in Babylonia the newly promulgated Mishnah which had just been issued in Palestine by the patriarch Judah *ca.* A.D. 200. Whatever old traditions and *ad hoc* decisions existed in Babylonia, the new Mishnah had irresistible appeal. Based upon a viable and supple exegetical method, it was organized according to logical categories, and, most important, was advertised as the very will of God revealed, along with the written Torah, by God to Moses at Mount Sinai and transmitted from that time to the present by faithful prophets, sages, and rabbis. Still a relatively new institution, the exilarchate was glad to associate itself and its administration with so grand a prestige as accrued to the Mishnah in the minds of those rabbis who accepted the rabbinical claim of its origin in the revelation of Sinai. Among these were the exilarch's own son Nathan; his relatives, Ḥiyya and Rav; and others close to him. He, too, therefore, was probably a believer. The exilarch claimed to be of the seed of David. How better to win the loyalty and conformity of ordinary people than to couple that claim with the equally impressive one: "In the Jewish courts we at last apply not merely the scattered, though hoary, traditions of our forefathers of the exile, but the whole revelation of Sinai itself."

In the decades after the redaction and promulgation of the Mishnah by the patriarch in Palestine, the exilarch gladly accepted its authority, and therefore hired men who would apply it—under exilarchic auspices to be sure. The rabbinical movement, small and possessing little influence and authority in Babylonia in the beginning, received the enthusiastic backing of the exilarch, who had earlier sent his representatives to the Palestinian schools. Whatever other schools there were must have either ceased to exist or begun to teach the Mishnah and its accompanying traditions, exegetical methods, and rules. In response the rabbis ruled that it was only with the authorization of the exilarch that one might judge cases in Jewish Babylonia. "Authorization" in rabbinic discourse meant actual bureaucratic appointment by the exilarch, and so an alliance was forged between the rabbis, needing political support, and the exilarch, requiring prestigious and qualified functionaries.

iv. MESSIAH VS. TORAH

How did the two groups—the exilarch and his circle on one side, and the rabbinical estate on the other—understand, themselves, and explain to others the power they exercised over the Jewish community at large? Two quite different claims of normative authority or legitimacy were put forward in Babylonian Judaism. Both were based upon myth, stories about or statements of ultimate reality in highly symbolic form. Although interrelated, the myths were different. One, the Torah-myth, served the purposes of the rabbis; the other, the Messiah-myth, was advanced by the exilarch.

The rabbis' political myth is examined in the following story (b. Giṭ. 62a) about Geniva, a rabbinical master of the second half of the third century who was finally put to death by the exilarch of the day, Mar 'Uqba:

R. Huna and R. Hisda were sitting, when Geniva happened by. One said to the other, "Let us arise before him, for he is master of Torah."

The other said, "Shall we arise before a man of division?"

Meanwhile he came, and said to them, "Peace be unto you, Kings, peace be unto you, Kings."

They said to him, "How do you know that rabbis are called kings?"

He said to them, "As it is said, *By me, kings rule*" (Prov. 8:15, referring to wisdom).

"And how do you know that a double greeting is given to kings?"

"As Rav Judah said in the name of Rav, 'How do you know that a double greeting is given to the king?' As it is said, *Then the spirit came upon Amasai who was chief of the thirty* (I Chron 12:18, continuing 'Peace, peace be upon you')."

They said to him, "Would you care for a bite with us?" He replied . . .

The story of his trial and execution is as follows (b. Giṭ. 7a):

Mar 'Uqba sent to R. Eleazar [ben Pedat], "Men are opposing me, and it is in my power to hand them over to the government. What is to be done?"

He drew a line and wrote to him, *"I said, I will take heed to my ways, that I sin not with my tongue, I will keep a curb upon my mouth while the wicked is before me* [Ps. 39:2], that is, even though the wicked is against me, I shall guard my mouth with a muzzle."

Again he said to him, "They are greatly troubling me, and I cannot overcome them."

He replied, *"Resign thyself unto the Lord and wait patiently for him* (Ps. 37:7) that is, wait for the Lord and he will bring them down prostrate before you. Arise early and stay late in the academy, and they will perish of themselves."

The matter had scarcely left the mouth of R. Eleazar when they placed Geniva in a collar to lead him to execution.

The difficulty Geniva gave the exilarch Mar 'Uqba was based on the relationship between the rabbi and the exilarch. Geniva and his party had said or done something the exilarch found extremely irritating, and the latter, having no capital jurisdiction over the Jews, handed him over to the Iranian government for punishment. The Iranian regime would, of course, properly support its functionary's authority.

Since the bulk of Geniva's reported sayings were quite standard rabbinical traditions, only the passage on the "double greeting" provides a hint of how he might have offended Mar 'Uqba. It may be supposed that he had publicly declared something the rabbis previously kept to themselves: their belief that the exilarch, who judged cases according to Persian law, derived his authority not from knowledge of the rabbinical traditions but from the support of a heathen government; that he collaborated in the affairs of that government; and that such a person was not really qualified to administer Jewry's affairs. Instead the rabbis felt that since they themselves were kings, they should rule.

This threat to the exilarchic position could have elicited only one response—to put the troublemaker out of the way. Until that could be arranged, the exilarch would have encouraged other rabbis to keep their distance from Geniva, despite his obvious mastery of traditions. Indeed, R. Huna and R. Ḥisda, who was Mar 'Uqba's teacher, were well aware of the dangers of associating with the "man of division." Their respect for his learning was tempered by their hesitation to have anything at all to do with him. Geniva for his part responded by quoting traditions deriving from their own master, Rav—traditions which they quite obviously did not know. By stressing their "kingship" he meant to point out the egregious quality of the relationship: they should not serve one lesser than themselves. They were rabbis, therefore kings, and Scripture had said so.

The exilarch's political myth is revealed in a saying by one of his own rabbinical adherents, Naḥman b. Jacob, who lived at the same time as Geniva. He stated (b. Sanh. 98b) :

"If [the messiah] is among the living, he is such a one as I, as it is said, *And their nobles shall be of themselves, and their governors shall proceed from the midst of them* (Jer. 30:21)."

As part of the exilarchate, Naḥman saw himself in an extraordinary light. Jeremiah refers to the time of the Messiah when the fortunes of Jacob will be restored. The restoration would be signified by the Jews' once again governing themselves.

Naḥman inferred that the rule of the exilarchate certified, and might in time mark the fulfillment of, that particular Messianic promise. Such a saying reflected the political theology of the exilarch. Being both scion of David and recognized governor of the Jews, the exilarch represented the fulfillment of prophetic hopes for the restoration of a Jewish monarch of the Davidic line. Hence his rule was legitimate and should be obeyed. Naḥman's citation of Jeremiah provides one of the few glimpses into the way the exilarch explained his rule to the Jews. It shows that not merely Persian approval and support, but a wholly "proper" basis in Jewish genealogy and history provided the theoretical foundation of his power. By contrast, the rabbis maintained that not Davidic overlordship, but full obedience to the Torah would signify the advent of Messianic rule.

The Davidic origins of the exilarch were first referred to in the time of Judah, the patriarch of Palestinian Jewry at the end of the second century A.D., in a colloquy between Judah and Ḥiyya (b. Hor. 11b):

Rabbi [Judah the Prince] inquired of R. Ḥiyya [a Babylonian related to the exilarch], "Is one like myself to bring a he-goat [as a sin-offering of a ruler, according to Lev. 4:23]?"

"You have your rival in Babylonia," he replied.

"The kings of Israel and the kings of the house of David," he objected, "bring sacrifices independently of one another."

"There," Ḥiyya replied, "they were not subordinate to one another. Here [in Palestine] we are subordinate to them [in Babylonia]."

R. Safra taught thus: Rabbi [Judah] inquired to R. Ḥiyya, "Is one like me to bring a he-goat?"

"There is the scepter, here is only the law-giver, as it was taught, *The scepter shall not depart from Judah*, refers to the Exilarch in Babylonia who rules Israel with the scepter, *nor the ruler's staff between his feet* [Gen. 49:10] refers to the grandchildren of Hillel who teach the Torah to Israel in public."

The reference to Gen. 49:10, *"The scepter shall not depart from Judah,"* is striking, for it shows that the Davidic claim was tied to the exercise of political authority. So far as the Palestinians were concerned, the exilarch's claim was taken as fact.

As earlier noted, the rabbis believed that, along with the written Torah, God had revealed to Moses at Mount Sinai an oral, unwritten Torah, which had been preserved and handed on from prophets to sages and finally to rabbis. Israel's life was to be shaped by divine revelation; the rabbis alone knew the full configuration of the will of God, and their claim to rule rested upon the belief in the oral Torah. They thus clashed with the exilarch, who, using equally theological terms, maintained that he was qualified to rule because he was descended from the seed of David. Moreover, rabbinic political theology ran counter to the widespread conviction of Jews that *anyone* holding political power over them had better be able to claim Davidic ancestry.

The rabbis authenticated their claim to power not only by their teaching of Torah, but also by their knowledge of the secrets of creation—including the names of God by which miracles may be produced, and the mysteries of astrology, medicine, and practical magic—and by their day-to-day conduct as a class of religious virtuosi and illuminati. For their schools they eagerly recruited students who would join with them in the task of studying the "whole Torah," and go forth afterward to exemplify and enforce its teaching among the ordinary people. They were seeking totally to reform the life of Israel so that it would conform to the Torah as they taught it. They believed that if Israel would live according to the will of "their Father in heaven," then no nation or race could rule over them, but the Anointed of God would do so. History as a succession of pagan empires would come to an end; Israel would live in peace in its own land; an endless age of prosperity because of Israel's reconciliation with God would follow. So the issues were not inconsiderable.

"How do you know that rabbis are called kings?" The reply is, "Scripture says, 'By me kings rule.'" Such was not the view of the exilarch, who wanted it to be believed that he ruled because he was heir of David. It is worth quoting the entire biblical passage (Prov. 8:15) to which Geniva made reference:

> By me kings rule
>     and rulers decree what is just
> By me princes rule
>     and nobles govern the earth.

This passage was part of a key proof text for the rabbinical schools, for in it, "Torah" (which they believed they alone properly expounded) is described as the beginning of the works of creation; as the foundation for right politics; and as the sole source of righteousness, justice, and knowledge. Torah came before creation, and so provided the design for the world. The chapter (Prov. 8:34-36) closes:

> Happy is the man who listens to me,
>     watching daily at my gates,

waiting beside my doors.
For he who finds me finds life
and obtains favor from the Lord;
But he who misses me injures himself;
all who hate me love death.

It was far more than a matter of power politics. When the rabbis read a reference to the gates and doors of Torah, they knew what it meant—the gates of their academies.

The crux of the matter was: How was redemption to be gained? The rabbis believed it was through a legal reformation of Israel. The exilarch and his relatives thought differently, for Naḥman supposed that their Davidic connection ought to prove sufficient in time to produce a Messiah, possibly even in their own day if God willed it. Redemption would proceed either from the academies or from the Davidides; the two were mutually exclusive. Beyond the concrete issues of the day, the question of redemption smoldered in the shadows, lending eschatological significance to a politics which was, from today's perspective, concerned with trivialities. "Torah" was central in the redemptive process. A legal reformation would effect "Torah" and so bring about the Messiah's coming. "All who hate me love death." The exilarchs were seen by their enemies as hating Torah. Had the exilarch subordinated himself to the academies and accepted their direction, the potential conflict between the opposing legacies might never have been realized.

But the exilarch had a powerful claim too. He was of David's seed, and from him or from one of his relatives would come the Messiah. That claim was probably far older and better established in the mind of Babylonian Jewry than that of the rabbis, and for better reasons. The exilarch had no reason to subordinate himself to the academy, and he had very good reason not to.

From the rabbis' perspective, the exilarch was a merely political figure, while they themselves were endowed with the sanctity deriving from Torah, revelation. In modern terms, they would have called themselves "the church" and the exilarch "the state." And—"By me, kings rule." But the exilarch's viewpoint could not have conformed to theirs. As far as he was concerned, his rule was as the surrogate of the Messiah; indeed his presence was the best assurance that the Messiah would one day come—and would come from his own household. Israel was not rejected by God as long as she

59

governed herself, and the exilarch's rule was therefore proof of the continued validity of the covenant, of the enduring Messianic hope; the scepter had *not* departed from Judah. *Not* a secular authority, the exilarch claimed to descend from David, to be the link between the rule of David in the ideal past and the rule of David in the ideal future. The Torah-myth thus came into conflict with the Messiah-myth.

It cannot be said, however, that the exilarch, a "merely political figure," was alone in making use of a religious myth for political purposes. The rabbis too sought to control political institutions—the courts and administrative agencies of Babylonian Jewry. They wanted to make use of those political institutions for religious purposes, that is, to coerce ordinary Jews to conform to the Torah as they taught it.

Both the rabbis and the exilarch claimed to be "the church" and therefore to be the state also. No distinction was recognized between politics and religion. If one ruled, it was because God wanted him to do so. If another obeyed, he obeyed heaven and revelation, not merely the arbitrary fiat of a temporarily powerful individual. Society should be governed by God's law; on this, everyone agreed. The issue was, Who knew that law? And who should be the one to interpret and apply it? Political argument was phrased in theological language, and only by accepting the claim of one party and rejecting that of the other can one be described as "the church," and the other as "the state." Political theory obviously was subsumed under the eschatological and Messianic issue: how is Israel to be saved?

The exilarch certainly expected that someday the Lord would send the Messiah, raising him up out of the house of the exilarch, related as it was to the Davidic family. That commonplace theory probably represented the older political view of both Babylonian and Palestinian Jewry. It was believed that redemption would come in God's own time, through David's descendant, and anyone presuming to exercise political authority over Jews had best begin with a claim to derive from the Davidic household. It is known that Davidic ancestry was alleged by practically every important Jewish figure in the political life of the late antiquity; included were the Hasmoneans, Jesus, the patriarchal family in Palestine, the exilarch —and even Herod!

In Iranian culture, it was conventional to claim to be an heir of the Achemenids, Cyrus and Darius, for example. The Parthians did so, not at the outset of their rule, but only in the first century when they found that military superiority no longer could sustain their throne. On the other hand, the Sasanians stated from the very outset that they were heirs of the Achemenids. Maintaining that the Parthians were illegitimate, the Sasanians asserted that they were the restorers of the ancient, rightful dynasty of Iran. The claim to be descended from a remote, glorious emperor was a widespread political convention in this time; what was strikingly unconventional was the rabbis' Torah-myth and its political expression.

It apparently was not sufficient for anyone to claim rulership because he had power, because he was wise, or because custom dictated it. Jewish politics revolved around the Messianic issue. Others could obey because it was expedient or merely necessary, but Jews would listen only to the Messiah's surrogate, obey only the word of God. In the humblest details of daily conduct they sought significance of grand, metahistorical dimensions. Ruling no government like other governments, Jews entered a fantasy in which what they did control, despite its worldly triviality, was believed to possess far greater significance than even the deeds of great and impressive empires held by others: "Others are ruled by the court of Ctesiphon, by the king of kings. We obey the King of kings of kings, the Holy One." The debate centered, therefore, on what obedience to God entailed—whether God's will was contained in the Torah of the rabbis or whether it was expressed through the rule of the exilarch, the scion of David. Theology imposed itself on politics probably because theology was all the Jews had left to render their politics worthwhile.

### v. Conflict of Myths

The practical conflict between the power of the exilarch and that of the rabbis may best be described in terms of an issue debated in the early fourth century: Should rabbis pay taxes?

The exilarch imposed and collected taxes, dividing them among Jews of various towns and groups, and transmitting them to the state on specified occasions. It would hardly enhance his authority if he could not impose his will upon everyone, including rabbis. Choosing to make the payment of the poll tax the decisive issue, the rabbis asserted that they were not like other Jews, but formed a special class which was subjected neither to the authority of the exilarch nor to the control of the state. For his part, the exilarch saw no reason to change the status quo of nearly three centuries' standing.

Why did rabbis choose just this time to claim exemption from taxation? A partial reason was that they were convinced they had no other correct course; furthermore, the time seemed promising. During the period from Shapur I's death in A.D. 273, to the end of the minority of Shapur II in about 325, the central government was distracted by disastrous foreign wars, the suppression of the Manichaeans, dynastic struggles every few years, and finally the centrifugal effects of the weak regency. When Shapur II came to power, his attention was drawn to international and military issues. The Sasanian government in his time never paid the Jews much attention while the revenues were forthcoming and nothing subversive happened. Both conditions were met. Subversion by the rabbis was not directed at the Sasanian government. So long as the full quota of head taxes was paid, it hardly mattered in the state who actually paid them or who did not. The Jewish question was an inconsequential local matter, and greater affairs of state must have occupied not only Shapur, who certainly was not even consulted on such a minor question, but also the ministers of Ctesiphon.

Had it been otherwise, the ministers of Shapur would have been perfectly well prepared to investigate anti-government activity and to punish those they thought guilty. The same satraps and Mobads who in the fourth century tortured Christian monks and nuns, priests, bishops, and laity of Babylonia and Adiabene for not paying taxes were quite capable of persecuting rabbis, if not the Jews as a group, had they thought it useful to the security of the state. They did nothing of the sort; presumably they saw no reason to.

Moreover, once the great persecution against the Christians had begun, in *ca.* 340, the exilarch could hardly have called to his aid those whose capacities for bloody mischief now stood fully revealed. Had he asked for state aid in suppressing the rabbinate as a class, he would have embittered the ordinary Jews against himself; and the record of rabbinical martyrdoms, accompanied by the conventional miracles done by both heavenly messengers and earthly saints, would have rendered him totally distasteful to common folk. So the exilarch at first was unwilling, and later quite unable to enlist the powers of the state. The state, unknowing and uninterested, paid attention to quite different matters. Still, in such a circumstance rebellion against the exilarch was a chancy thing. The rabbis took that chance.

The exilarch was prepared to grant unusual favors to the rabbis as an estate. They had special privileges at court; they were given advantages in marketing their produce. The exilarch was quoted as instructing Rava to see whether a certain man who was claiming rabbinical status was really a scholar. If so, Rava was to reserve a market privilege for him, so that he might sell his produce before others. Since the rabbis staffed exilarchic courts, it certainly was advantageous to protect them.

The rabbis' claim to be exempt from the poll tax was quite another matter, however. The exilarch could not exempt rabbis from the poll tax. One of the principal guarantees of continued peace for the Jewish community was the efficient collection of taxes, and the exilarch himself would have had to make up any deficit. All he could do was shift the burden of taxes to others, so that the rabbis' share would devolve upon ordinary Jews. He was not ready to do so, and it is extremely unlikely that ordinary people would have wanted him to. The tax rates already were so high that poor people struggled to find the money to pay them. References abound to people's selling their property, or themselves into slavery, to raise the necessary money. The state could not afford to compromise. War was necessary to protect its territory, including first and foremost Babylonia itself. Armies were expensive, and contributions were required of everyone, particularly of those who lived in so rich and fertile a region. Moreover, those living closest to the capital were least able to evade the taxes. So the exilarch could hardly accede to the rabbis' demand. The Iranians would not allow the lightening of taxes; the ordinary Jews could not bear an additional burden if it were shifted to them.

The rabbis' claim of tax-exemption was phrased in scriptural terms. They were certain that from most ancient times rabbis were not supposed to pay taxes and that it would be a transgression of scriptural precedent if they now did so. A positive claim was made by R. Naḥman b. Isaac (b. B.B. 8a) :

R. Naḥman b. R. Ḥisda [an exilarchic representative] applied the head-tax to the sages.

R. Naḥman b. Isaac said to him, "You have transgressed against the teachings of the Torah, the Prophets, and the Writings. Against the Torah, as it is written, *Although he loves the people, all his saints are in your hand* (Deut. 33:3).

"You have transgressed against the Prophets, as it is written, *Even when they study* [lit.: Give] *among the nations, now I shall gather them, and a few of them shall be free from the burden of kings and princes* (Hosea 8:10).

"You have transgressed against the Writings, as it is written, *It shall not be lawful to impose upon them* [priests and Levites] *minda, belo, and halakh* (Ezra 7:24), and Rav Judah explained, '*Minda* means the portion of the king, *belo* is the poll-tax, and *halakh* is the *annona* [corvée].'"

The several Scriptures are not of equal weight. The passage in Deuteronomy suggests that "his saints" (believed by the rabbis to be themselves) are in God's hand. Therefore, they do not require the protection of walls or armies and should not have to pay for them. Likewise, R. Judah b. Ezekiel had said that everyone must contribute to the building of doors for the town walls and gates except rabbis, who do not require the protection of walls and gates. The meaning of the passage in Hosea is quite clear: when the Jews study the Torah among the gentiles (i.e., in Babylonia), a few should not have to pay taxes; and these few, quite obviously, are the rabbis. The citation from Ezra explicitly states that priests do not have to pay the "portion of the king" or the poll tax. What was not made explicit, because everyone in the schools knew it, was that the rabbis believed they had inherited the rights and privileges of the priesthood, since study of Torah was now equivalent to the priestly offerings in Temple times. Therefore, according to Artaxerxes' order reported by Ezra, rabbis do not have to pay the head tax. This was plainly stated in Scripture, and the rabbis felt it was beyond question. Even the Iranian government should not impose the poll tax on them, they supposed. Rava threatened that the rabbis would apostasize (b. Ned. 62b):

Rava said, "It is permitted for a rabbinical disciple to say, 'I will not pay the toll-tax,' as it is written, *It shall not be lawful to impose minda, belo, or halakh*" (Ezra 7:24).

Rava moreover stated, "A rabbinical disciple is permitted to say, 'I am a servant of fire and do not pay the poll tax.'"

What is the reason? It is only said in order to drive away a lion.

Rava's remarkable saying that a rabbinical disciple could lie to evade the poll tax or even deny that he was a Jew, tells nothing about what would have happened had he done so. The tax-collectors in the Jewish community were Jews, not Iranians. What Rava has in mind was a Jew telling the Jewish collector that he was an apostate. There might have been an implied threat: "If you do not leave me alone, I shall become a servant of fire." It is doubtful that Rava imagined a rabbinical disciple would make such an assertion before a Mobad, who knew full well how to assess such a claim. His thought was that it was so wrong to collect the poll tax from rabbis, that the disciples could perjure themselves or even pretend to commit overt apostasy. It was a very strong assertion.

The only sources currently available do not reveal what the exilarch said or did in response to the rabbinical tax rebellion. If Torah, Prophecy, and Writings are brought to testify, and public apostasy theoretically was permitted to a rabbinical disciple, one can hardly suppose that rabbis were not under pressure. The greater likelihood is that they paid their tax but resisted as power- fully as they could through their most effective weapons—ascription of their tax exemption to Moses, Hosea, and Artaxerxes, and public announcements of permission to evade the taxes by any means. The exilarch exerted great pressure, because he both had to and wanted to. The vehemence of the rabbis' traditions on the subject must be interpreted as evidence of his success.

It is not known whether R. Naḥman b. Isaac ever managed to intimidate R. Naḥman b. R. Ḥisda, or, for that matter, whether any young rabbinical disciples actually lied to the tax-collectors. It is known, however, that Shapur II's police from A.D. 339 to 379 exe- cuted Christian tax-resisters. Since there is no evidence of "martyr- dom" of rabbis because of nonpayment of taxes, it is very likely that there was none. The rabbis protested, but they must have paid. To the exilarch, that would have been all that really mattered.

But the rabbis would have been embittered not only because they had lost money, which would have especially bothered the poorer ones, but also because they were forced to transgress their religious convictions about their own rights and privileges. Their view of the sanctity of the rabbinate is clear: they were the "saints" in God's hand. It was a sin for them to pay the poll tax, and it was a still greater sin for the exilarch to force them to do so.

The exilarch had to respond publicly to the criticism and dis- loyalty of hostile elements in the rabbinate. His response probably would have taken the form of propaganda which would have been not less venomous than that of the rabbis. To begin with, he would have stressed his descent from the house of David, for that was the foundation of his politics. He would, moreover, have alluded to the cost to other Jews of the rabbinical tax exemption and maintained that the rabbis refused to pay their fair share of the rising imposts. The rabbis wanted to establish a second Jewish government, which the Persians would never allow. "In these troubled times, when Christians are giving evidence of what happens to minority-communities that fall afoul of the state," the exilarch would have pointed out, "it will not pay to solicit Persian hostility!"

Furthermore, according to the exilarch, the condition of the Jews themselves would have provided the best testimony to the soundness of exilarchic rule: "Consider the fact that while others are persecuted, Jews are secure. Chaos reigns everywhere, but at home there is order, or as much order as responsible government can bring when faced with such dissident, provocative elements." The exilarch could therefore have concluded his message by asking, "How many wish to enslave themselves to pay heavier taxes so that rabbis may now enjoy the full benefit of their private, fantastic, and self-serving scriptural exegesis? Not all rabbis, to be sure, but only a minority of them are guilty of such intended subversion. Most of them remain loyal to the house of David and its living representative." The living representative was, of course, the exilarch himself.

Three centuries earlier, Yoḥanan b. Zakkai, excluded from the bastions of power in Jerusalem and displeased with the Temple priesthood's administration of its holy office, had found a suitable polemic in the words of Qohelet 4:18, *Guard your foot when you go to the house of God and be ready to hearken.* He said that it was better to listen to the words of the wise than to offer the sacrifices of fools, meaning the ancient priesthood. Now his words found an echo in the saying attributed to Rava (b. Ber. 23a):

*And be ready to listen.* Rava said, "Be ready to listen to the words of the sages, for if they sin, they bring an offering and carry out penance." *It is better than when fools give.* "Do you be like fools who sin and bring an offering, but do not do penance."

vi. RECONCILIATION

During the next fifty years, from *ca.* 330 to *ca.* 380, the exilarch was able to reassert complete control over the rabbinical schools. At the same time, however, he made certain that his functionaries and heirs received an excellent rabbinical education. So in effect he capitulated by becoming a rabbi himself, that is, by getting a sound knowledge of the Torah as taught by rabbis. But he insisted that the schools where Jews became rabbis remain under his very close supervision. No true victor can therefore be designated in the struggle for power in the Jewish community. The rabbis rabbinized the exilarchate; the exilarch exercised substantial control over the rabbinate.

These two groups suffered in a disaster which occurred during the reign of the Sasanian emperor Peroz, when both leading rabbis and the exilarch, believing the Messiah would come in 468—four hundred years after the destruction of Jerusalem—foolishly acted upon the consequences of that belief. Jewish government was wiped out. It was an ironic denouement. The rabbis followed the exilarch's Messianism and endorsed it. If, therefore, the exilarch was "rabbinized," the rabbis were "Messianized." The two theories were united; the two parties suffered together.

A detailed examination of this disaster will set into perspective the consideration of power within Babylonian Judaism. The essential weakness of the Jewish community and all its institutions, including both the exilarchate and the rabbinate, become apparent in this study. Until ca. A.D. 450, Judaism had been a licit religion. After that time, for close to half a century, Judaism was treated as an illicit religion, and some Jews were punished for practicing it. To find a similarly severe crisis one has to look backward to the brief but vicious Hadrianic repression following the Bar Kokhba War. First a review of the Peroz catastrophe as it appears in several sources and traditions:

R. Naḥman b. R. Huna died in the year 455 A.D. Then a persecution took place, for Yazdagird [the Iranian king of kings] decreed to annul the Sabbath.

(*Letter of R. Sherira Gaon*, ed. B. M. Lewin
[Haifa, 1921], pp. 94, 1. 12-13; 95, 1. 1-2)

In the year 455 R. Naḥman b. R. Huna died. And Argazur [sic!] the King of the Persians decreed against our fathers that they profane Sabbaths. In the year 468 Rabbah b. R. Ashi died. In the year 471 R. Ḥama son of Rava died. Huna b. Mar Zuṭra the exilarch was killed, and the Jews were given over to the government. In the year 467 the schools were destroyed. And they decreed against the Jews to be subject to Persian law. And Rabbah Tosfa'ah died.

(*Seder Tannaim ve Amoraim*, ed. M. Grosberg
[London, 1908], Chapter II, p. 65)

A later tradition provides the following account of the insertion of the *Shema'* in the *Qedushah*, the sanctification-prayer:

Because in the time of R. Naḥman, Yuzgard [sic!] the king of Persia decreed that the *Shema'* should not be read. Forthwith what did the sages of that generation do? They decreed to include it in the midst of every *Qedushah.* . . . And why did they decree to say it by swallowing [= inclusion elsewhere]? So that the *Shema'* should not be forgotten by the children. And they sought mercy from heaven. Thereupon a serpent came at noonday and swallowed Yuzgard the king in his bed, and the decree was annulled.

The *Letter of R. Sherira* further states that an important rabbi died in 459 at the time of the persecution decreed by Yazdagird.

Rabbana Amemar bar Mar Yenuqa, Huna Mar bar R. Ashi the exilarch, and Mesharshia b. Peqod were imprisoned. On the 18th day of Ṭevet, Huna bar Mar Zuṭra the *Nasi* [= exilarch] and Mesharshia were killed, and in Adar of the same year Rabbana Amemar bar Mar Yenuqa was killed.

And in the year 470 all the synagogues in Babylonia were closed, and the children of the Jews were seized by the Magi.

(*Letter of R. Sherira Gaon*,
pp. 96, 1. 14-16; 95, 1. 1-9)

The same event appears in the *Book of Tradition* (*Sefer HaQabbalah*) of Abraham ibn Daud:

Before this [the Moslem conquest], however, the Almighty, blessed be He, had turned their heart to hate His people, so that the Persian king seized three Jewish notables: Amemar bar Mar Yanqa bar Mar Zuṭra, the colleague of R. Ashi, R. Mesharshia, and the exilarch, whose name was Huna Mar, and put them to death. He also seized Jewish youths and compelled them to leave the fold.

(*The Book of Tradition* [Philadelphia: Jewish Publication
Society of America, 1968], ed. and trans.
Gerson D. Cohen, IV, 1. 158-64, pp. 41-42)

68

According to the Iranian historian Hamza Iṣfahani, in the eleventh year of Peroz' reign (468), Jews of Iṣfahan flayed two Magi (Zoroastrian priests) alive. As a result, half the Jewish population of Iṣfahan was slaughtered, and the children were handed over to the service of the fire-temple at Harvan.

What is the import of these medieval accounts? It is known that Yazdagird II and Peroz persecuted Christianity. Just as they directed their efforts against priests, nuns, and monks, so in the Jewish case they are said to have imprisoned and then put to death both rabbis, particularly those who were heads of schools, and the exilarch. Since the Christian case was primarily a religious persecution, without the usual attribution of political motives, it is striking that the Jewish accounts report decrees against keeping the Sabbath, the conduct of schools, and similar, fundamental Jewish religious practices, not to mention the abolition of Jewish self-government. So the persecutions of the two religious communities exhibit similar qualities.

Moreover, the independent account from Iṣfahan provides a measure of verification for the Jewish stories. For example, the detail about seizure of Jewish children for Mazdean purposes appears in both Jewish and Iranian traditions. But of still greater significance in the Iṣfahan version is the reason for the persecution. Jewish and Christian traditions claim that it was directed against their religious practices, and therefore presumably was motivated by religious "fanaticism"; the Iranian story is that Jews had mistreated Magi and as a result were punished. Iranians viewed the "persecution" as a *local* action against the malfeasance of a *local* community.

There are stories available from Christian sources of Christian saints burning down fire-temples during the reign of Yazdagird I, *ca.* A.D. 410. It is by no means incredible that Jews did something of the same sort in Iṣfahan. The Christians acted because they thought Yazdagird I would follow the path of Constantine and become a Christian.

The Jews had a tradition that the Messiah could come in the year 468, that is, four hundred years after the destruction of the Temple:

Said R. Ḥanina, "From the year 400 after the destruction [of the Temple, dated by the rabbis in 68] if someone says to you, 'Buy a field worth a thousand *denarii* for one *denar*,' do not buy it."

In a *beraita* we learn, "From the year 4231 of the Creation of the World

69

onward [= A.D. 471], if someone says to you, 'Buy a field worth a thousand *denarii* for a *denar,*' do not buy it."

(b. A. Z. 9b)

R. Ḥanina lived in the third century in Palestine, but it is known that his tradition was preserved in the Babylonian schools a century and a half later. Some Jews, including leading rabbis, expected the Messiah to come in 468 or shortly thereafter, and the preliminary destruction of pagan temples and murder of their priests followed as a consequence of such a belief. No information is currently available on what happened, if anything, in Iṣfahan in 468. But it is plausible that some Jews would have done what later Iranian tradition claimed they did. If so, the local pogrom would have been a natural result.

It is puzzling that the state engaged in such a far-reaching repression of Judaism as a religion. If Magi went so far as to seize Jews and interrogate them about religious matters, investigate and legislate concerning the content of Jewish worship, close synagogues, snatch away Jewish children, and the like, and if the state supported these actions, surely some motive or provocation far more profound than political or economic necessity must have been at hand. And if Jews provoked these severe repressions, as the Iṣfahani tradition says they did, they surely must have had a considerable reason.

In the background of every Jewish act of political or religious violence lies the Messianic expectation. Therefore the conviction that the Messiah would come in 468 or in 471 must be taken very seriously. In the days of Shapur II, in 362-363, a movement similar to that in Iṣfahani took shape in Maḥoza, and the king was compelled to send troops to massacre the Messianists. Later more movements appeared, coalescing around local figures in Babylonia and Mesopotamia, as well as in Byzantine territories. In the second and third decades of the fifth century, Messianic movements were rampant both in Jewish Palestine and in the Greek diaspora. Obviously Messianism constituted a powerful force in Babylonian Judaism, and Jewish Messianists invariably took active measures in support of their convictions. A bloody war was fought in Hadrianic times when they had believed Bar Kokhba to be the Messiah (a belief that had been confirmed by some rabbis). The natural result of this religion was repression not only of the war but also of those Judaic religious practices which the Romans believed had caused it.

70

Similarly, when the Iranians conquered Jerusalem in A.D. 614, Palestinian Jews again believed the Messiah was about to come. As a consequence of the capture of Jerusalem, they murdered many local Christians, particularly the religious.

The fact that the Sabbath was prohibited, certain central prayers were outlawed, and important rabbis—including the exilarch himself—were put to death in the years between *ca.* 455 and *ca.* 475, seems to be illuminated by the Messianic expectations attached to this period. Whatever the religious convictions of Yazdagird and Peroz, Jews may well have followed the dictates of their *own* piety, with disastrous results. The earlier persecutions combined with the older tradition about what would happen in 468 served to arouse this expectation. It was a self-fulfilling prophecy. The involvement and death of the exilarch is particularly striking, because the rabbis had taught (and presumably the exilarch did as well) that the Messiah would come forth from the Davidic household of the exilarch. If the exilarch was implicated in a rebellion, his government would naturally have been outlawed.

The disaster of 468 is a fitting end to this account of the institutions and theories of power in Babylonian Judaism. It underlines how little actual power was in the hands of Jews; they could not even control their own destiny. So far as the myths that explained and shaped history served to reconcile the Jews to their situation of weakness, they proved adaptive and functional. But when those myths led to the expectation that Jews might take into their own hands the worldly side of the Messianic task, they became dysfunctional and destructive. The competition between exilarch and rabbi, therefore, was in accord with the political realities of Jewish life. It focused partisan energies upon internal issues and thus kept the community out of trouble. But the reconciliation between the two released those energies, bringing catastrophe.

# Chapter Three

---

# Myth

### i. The Common Myth of the Middle East

Myths—the beliefs the people held about supernatural reality and the stories they told to embody, convey, or enact those beliefs—were represented in two discrete sources: first, the Babylonian Talmud and second, the magical bowls, dating to the fifth or sixth century A.D., which were discovered at the northern town of Nippur. Placed in houses as protection against demons, the bowls contained substantial inscriptions. Many were written by Jewish magicians, and some of their clients were Jewish.

What was it that concerned those clients? Let us summarize the messages of some of the inscriptions. Geyonai bar Mami was disturbed by liliths (female demons) in his bedroom. Babanos bar Qayomta and his wife Saradust b. Shirin were bothered by liliths in their dreams at night. Dadbeh bar Asmanduch and his wife, sons, and daughters sought general protection; they wished to be preserved from demons, devils, plagues, satans, curses, liliths, and tormentors. Komesh, daughter of Maḥlaphta, divorced a lilith. Berik-Yahbeh bar Mame and Ispandarmed bound lilith not to come, using the words of the *Shemaʿ* as part of a charm. Dinoi bar Ispandarmed sealed his house, wife, and children from the influence of the Tormentor and from evil dreams. Jesus the healer was called upon to seal the house of Mihr-hormizd bar Mami. Geniva bought a charm against evil spirits. Mazdewai daughter of Imma Salma and Beryl the son of Imma, her husband, used a bowl to preserve them in life

72

and to prevent demons from doing them harm. Babai b. Maḥlapta's house was afflicted with ghosts, and these had to be exorcised. The evil Zgus was in Yannai b. Zekhut, and had to be driven out or frightened away.

No peculiarly "Jewish" concerns appear. The things that bothered these Jews with Iranian and Syriac names equally afflicted their gentile neighbors. The means of healing these afflictions differed in no way from one community to the other. Gentiles and Jews alike wanted to be saved from demons and from illnesses, to exorcise ghosts, and, especially, to preserve the happiness of their marital life. Both groups believed demons had a particularly ill effect on these matters, and both looked forward to a salvation which consisted of good health, sexual satisfaction, and normal daily life unmarred by inexplicable accidents or bad luck. No one seems to have enjoyed an abundance of such blessings.

Just as the human concerns of the clients were held in common, so the magic to which they resorted was international and universal, transcending ethnic and political borders. The substratum of all religious communities of the Middle East exhibits a uniform mythic structure: belief in demons, angels, and holy men; hope for miracles attained through merits, prayers, incantations, or magic; fantasies about an unseen world which some men might have power to control. The common "faith" pertained primarily to this-worldly concerns, although it alluded to other-worldly powers. Rabbinic Judaism, by contrast, set for itself both this-worldly and other-worldly goals, aiming at the salvation of Israel and the world-to-come as much as at health, prosperity, and control of nature in this world. The chief concerns of the international myth were commonplace, yet personal; universal, yet individual. Those of the rabbis were primarily particular to the Jews, communal and collective.

### ii.   MOSES-PIETY: MOSES "OUR RABBI"

The encompassing myth revealed in the pages of the Babylonian Talmud centered upon the figure of Moses and could be called the story of the Moses-piety of the rabbis. That story related Moses' disclosure of a dual revelation, or Torah, at Mount Sinai—one in writing, the other handed orally from master to disciple. The whole Torah—oral and written—contained the design for the universe, the divine architect's plan for reality. It was to be studied, therefore, not merely for information, but as an act of piety and reverence for the divine lawgiver. Just as God had taught Torah to Moses, so the rabbi, modeling his life after Moses "our rabbi," taught his own disciple. In "studying Torah," and even more so in effecting it in the lives of Israel, the rabbi thus imitated God. Following the model of the "school" in heaven, the schools for Torah-study brought together masters and disciples and preserved the ancient traditions.

The most striking aspect of these schools was the rabbis' conception that in them lived holy men, men who more accurately than anyone else conformed to the image of God conveyed by divine revelation through the Torah of Moses our rabbi. The schools were not holy places in the sense that pious people made pilgrimages to them or that miracles were supposed to take place there, although pilgrimages were made and miracle-stories were told in a scholastic setting. The schools were holy because there men achieved sainthood through study of Torah and imitation of the conduct of the masters. In doing so, they conformed to the heavenly paradigm, the Torah, believed to have been created by God "in his image," revealed at Sinai, and handed down to their own teachers. Thus obedience to the teachings of the rabbis led not merely to ethical or moral goodness, but to holiness or sainthood. Discussion of legal traditions, rather than ascetic disciplines or long periods of fasting and prayer, was the way to holiness.

If the masters and disciples obeyed the divine teaching of Moses our rabbi as they surely believed that they did, then their society, the school, would replicate on earth the heavenly academy, just as the disciple would incarnate the heavenly model of Moses our rabbi. The rabbis believed that Moses was a rabbi, that God donned phylacteries, and that the heavenly court studied Torah precisely as did the earthly one. These beliefs today may be seen as projections of rabbinical values onto heaven, but the rabbis believed that they themselves were projections of heavenly values onto earth. That is not to suggest that rabbis thought of themselves as consubstantial with the Divinity. On the contrary, the distinction between the master of Torah and the Giver of Torah was carefully preserved.

iii.   ACADEMY ON EARTH AND IN HEAVEN

The Jews believed that the affairs of the schools were directly supervised from heaven. It was said, for example, that when Rava died, R. Ashi was born. Likewise Huna b. Nathan could not become exilarch while R. Ashi was still alive, for one "sovereignty" could not begin before another one had concluded. This view was explicitly attributed to the angel of death. While the actual chronology of Rava and R. Ashi is highly dubious, the conviction revealed is significant: Heaven arranged things so that great leadership would neither cease from the schools nor conflict in time.

[Abaye had ridiculed the view that one may cut off palm-branches during the festival week.] R. Ashi had a forest in Shelania'. He went to cut it down during the festival week.

R. Shila of Shelania' said to R. Ashi, "What is your opinion? . . . [Do you rely on an opinion contrary to Abaye? But Abaye ridiculed that opinion.]"

He said to him, "I have not heard it." [That is to say, it is not reasonable to me.]

The hatchet then slipped [from the heft] as if to cut off his leg. He left off his task and returned [after the festival week].

(b. M.Q. 12b)

The sages fully expected that the forces of nature would conspire to reveal, then to enforce, the correct view of the law. They felt certain of a close correspondence between the fate of man and his moral character. It was dangerous to anger a rabbi, for heaven would exact vengeance:

Once a man came and appeared before Rav and asked him, "What is [the legal status of a child] where an idolater or a slave had intercourse with the daughter of an Israelite?"

"The child is legitimate," the master replied.

"Give me then your daughter," said the man.

"I will not give her to you." [Rav did not regard the man as a worthy son-in-law.]

Said Shimi b. Ḥiyya to Rav, "People say that in Media, a camel can dance on a *qav* [square]. Here is the *qav*, here is the camel and here is Media, but there is no dancing!" [Why not put the ruling into practice?]

"Had he been equal to Joshua ben Nun, I would not have given him my daughter," the Master replied.

"Had he been like Joshua the son of Nun," the other retorted, "others would have given him their daughters, if the Master had not given his, but with this man, if the Master will not give him, others also will not give him."

As the man refused to go away [Rav] fixed his eye upon him and he died.

(b. Yev. 45a)

75

Even the rabbis' graves were venerated by the people:

It was the practice of people to take earth from Rav's grave and apply
it on the first day of an attack of fever. When Samuel was told of it
[that people were using an object belonging to the dead, which is for-
bidden], he said, "They do well; it is natural soil, and natural soil does
not become forbidden, for it is written, *And he cast the dust thereof upon
the graves of the common people* (II Kings 23:6), thus he compares the
graves of the common people to idols. Just as idols [are] not forbidden
when they are 'attached' [to the earth], for it is written, *Ye shall utterly
destroy all the places . . . upon the high mountains* (Deut. 12:2). i.e.,
their gods, which are *upon* the high mountains, but not the *mountains*
which themselves are their gods; so here too, what is 'attached' is not
forbidden."

(b. Sanh. 47b)

Samuel's exegesis thus permitted a practice which the people must
have regarded as meritorious, but which the rabbis could not have
approved if asked *ab initio* for permission. That the graves of the
sages were venerated suggests that they were believed to possess
power, or mana, not ordinarily found in other men. They were not
merely teachers and judges, therefore, but "holy men."

The following story provides an insight into the way in which
rabbis conceived of their relationship to heaven and used their
magical and Torah power:

R. Kahana said that R. Hama son of the daughter of Hama told him
that Rabbah b. Nahmani died on account of persecution:
Informers testified against him at court.
They said, "There is a certain man among the Jews who keeps twelve
thousand men of Israel from paying the royal head-tax a month in the
summer and a month in the winter. The court sent a royal messenger
after him, but he did not find Rabbah.
Rabbah fled from Pumbedita to 'Aqra', from 'Aqra' to 'Agma', and
from 'Agma' to Shehin, and from Shehin to Zerifa, and from Zerifa to
'Aina' deMayim, and from 'Aina' deMayim to Pumbedita. In Pumbedita
the messenger found him.
The royal messenger happened upon the hostel of Rabbah. They brought
the messenger a tray, gave him two cups [a way of calling up demons],
then removed the tray. His face was turned backward.
It was said to Rabbah, "What shall we do for him? He is a royal
messenger."

76

Rabbah replied, "Bring him a tray and give him one glass, then remove the tray and he will be healed."

They did so and the messenger was healed.

The agent said, "I am quite sure that the man I seek is here."

He searched and found Rabbah.

The detective said, "I shall leave here. If they kill me, I shall not reveal him, but if they torture me, I shall reveal him."

They brought Rabbah before him. He led Rabbah up to a chamber and locked the door before him. Rabbah prayed and the wall broke down. He fled to 'Agma'.

Rabbah was sitting on the trunk of a palm and studying. In the heavenly academy they were [then] arguing thus, "If a bright spot precedes a white hair, it is unclean, and if the white hair precedes the bright spot, it is clean. When in doubt, the Holy One, blessed be He, says it is clean, and the entire heavenly academy say it is unclean. Who will decide the matter? Let Rabbah b. Naḥmani decide it, for Rabbah b. Naḥmani said, 'I am uniquely qualified to decide cases of law relating to leprosy and tents.'"

The heavenly court sent a messenger after him. The angel of death could not come near him, because his mouth did not cease from repeating words of Torah [which kept the angel of death away].

Meanwhile a wind blew and caused a rustling in the branches. Rabbah feared that was a band of cavalry.

He said, "Let my soul die, but let me not be given into the hand of the government."

While dying, Rabbah said, "Clean, clean!"

A heavenly echo went forth and said, "Happy are you, Rabbah b. Naḥmani, that your body is clean, and your soul went forth in [speaking of] cleanness."

A slip of paper fell from heaven into Pumbedita [on which was written], "Rabbah b. Naḥmani has been summoned to the heavenly academy."

Abaye and Rava and all the rabbis went out to attend to him, but they did not know his place [where his body was lying]. They went to 'Agma' and saw birds hovering and overshadowing [the corpse]. They said, "So he is there." They mourned for him three days and three nights.

A slip of paper fell, "Whoever holds aloof [from lamenting] will be under a ban."

They mourned seven more days.

A slip of paper fell, "Go home in peace."

On that day, a hurricane lifted a Tai [Arab] who was riding a camel, from one side of the Papa canal to the other. The Arab said, "What is this?"

He was told, "Rabbah b. Naḥmani has died."

He cried, "Lord of the World! The whole world is yours, and Rabbah

b. Naḥmani is yours. You are Rabbah's and Rabbah is yours. Why do you destroy the world!" The storm subsided.

(b. B.M. 86a)

The rabbis thus conceived that on earth they studied Torah just as God, the angels, and Moses our rabbi did in heaven. The heavenly schoolmen were even aware of Babylonian scholastic discussions, so they required Rabbah's information about an aspect of purity-taboos. This conception must be interpreted by reference to the belief that the man truly made in the divine image was the rabbi; he embodied revelation—both oral and written—and all his actions constituted paradigms that were not merely correct, but actually heavenly. Rabbis, it shall be seen, could create and destroy men because they were righteous, free of sin, or otherwise holy, and so enjoyed exceptional grace from heaven. It follows that Torah was held to be a source of supernatural power. The rabbis controlled the power of Torah because of their mastery of its contents. They furthermore used their own mastery of Torah quite independent of heavenly action. They could issue blessings and curses, create men and animals, and were masters of witchcraft, incantations, and amulets. They could communicate with heaven. Their Torah was sufficiently effective to thwart the action of demons. However much they disapproved of other people's magic, they themselves were expected to do the things magicians did.

A further central conception set rabbinic Judaism apart from Manichaeism, Mazdaism, Oriental Christianity, and other contemporary cults: it was not expected that the masses would assume the obligations of or attain to the supernatural skills of Manichaean Elect, Mazdean Magi, Christian nuns and monks, or the religious virtuosi and cultic specialists of other groups. All Jews, however, were expected to become rabbis. The rabbis wanted to transform the entire Jewish community into an academy where the whole Torah was studied and kept.

These beliefs aid in understanding the rabbis' view that Israel would be redeemed through Torah. Because Israel had sinned, it was punished by being given over into the hands of earthly empires; when it atoned, it would be removed from their power. The means of this atonement or reconciliation were study of Torah, practice of commandments, and doing good deeds. These would transform each Jew into a rabbi, hence into a saint. When all Jews had become

78

rabbis, they then would no longer lie within the power of history. The Messiah would come. So redemption depended upon the "rabbinization" of all Israel, that is, upon the attainment by all Jewry of a full and complete embodiment of revelation or Torah, thus achieving a perfect replica of heaven. When Israel on earth became such a replica, it would be able, as a righteous, holy, saintly community, to exercise the supernatural power of Torah, just as some rabbis were already doing. With access to the consequent theurgical capacities, redemption would naturally follow.

### iv.  THE RABBI AS A HOLY MAN

The rabbi was the authority on theology, including the structure and order of the supernatural world. He knew the secret names of God and the secrets of the divine "chariot"—the heavens—and of creation. If extraordinarily pious, he might even see the face of the *Shekhinah,* the presence of God; in any event, the *Shekhinah* was present in the rabbinical schools. The rabbi overcame the evil impulse which dominated ordinary men and was consequently less liable to suffering, misfortune, and sickness. He was able to pray effectively because he knew the proper times and forms of prayer. Moreover, the efficacy of his prayers was heightened by his purity, holiness, and other merits, which in turn derived from his knowledge of the secrets of Torah and his consequent particular observances. He could bring rain or cause drought. His blessings brought fertility, and his curse, death. He was apt to be visited by angels and to receive messages from them. He could see and talk with demons and could also communicate with the dead. He was an authority on the interpretation of omens and dreams, the means of averting witchcraft, incantations for cures, knot-tying (for phylacteries), and the manufacture and use of amulets. In anthropological terms, he was a medicine man. If a modern anthropologist were able to spend a few years in ancient Pumbedita, Sura, or Nehardea to study the social role of the rabbi, his resultant book would certainly be called something like *The Lawyer-Magicians of Babylonia.*

Here, however, an important distinction must be made. The fact that the rabbis performed the functions and claimed the powers characteristic, in primitive societies, of magicians might justify a modern anthropologist in applying to them that term, but it does not prove that they applied the term to themselves or would have approved its application. In fact the rabbis would not have regarded their power as magical or the Torah as a source of magic (although some did practice magic on the side). The dividing line between true religion and magic was clearly drawn and widely recognized, and, by virtue of that recognition, became a social reality. What was approved by society—in this case, the schools—required by custom, and unquestionably seen as part of the established religion, was usually thought to be in no way magical. Abaye said:

"The sorcerer who insists upon exact paraphernalia [noting different properties of different kinds of magic] works through demons. He who does not, works by pure enchantment. . . .

"The laws of sorcerers are like those of the Sabbath: certain actions are punished by stoning, some are exempt from punishment, yet forbidden, whilst others are entirely permitted. Thus: if one actually performs magic, he is stoned; if he merely creates an illusion, he is exempt, yet it is forbidden." . . .

What is entirely permitted?

Such as [the magic] performed by R. Ḥanina and R. 'Oshaia, who spent every Sabbath eve in studying the Laws of Creation, by means of which they created a third-grown calf and ate it.

(b. Sanh. 67b)

One may suppose that "magic" was permitted if performed by the rabbis. Working through demons and enchantment may be no different to modern eyes from studying the "Laws of Creation" and applying them. But the distinction was important to Abaye. This distinction has been best illustrated by Morton Smith, professor of history at Columbia University, in an unpublished lecture:

In antiquity, the practice of magic was a criminal offense and the term "magician" was a term of abuse. It still is, but the connotation has changed. It now primarily connotes fraud. Then the notion was that of social subversion. The efficacy of magic was almost universally believed and the magician was conceived of as a man who, by acquiring supernatural powers, had become a potential danger to the established authority and to the order that they sought to maintain. Consequently magic was widely practiced but rarely admitted.

For Judaism there was a further limiting factor in the dogma that there was no god save the Lord. This did not lead to a denial of the efficacy of pagan magic nor did it prevent Jews from using the same magical practices as pagans. On the contrary, the Jews were famous as magicians, as Josephus says. And new discoveries show that as late as the fourth and fifth centuries Jews, steeped in the Old Testament and thoroughly at home in the Synagogue, were composing a magician's handbook which listed pagan deities and prescribed prayers and sacrifices to be offered to them in magical ceremonies. Among the prayers there is an invocation of Helios in transliterated Greek; and the conclusion comes upon reaching the Seventh Heaven with a celebration of Yahweh as the supreme God.

At least the more scrupulous of the Jews distinguished their marvels as performed by the power of the supreme God from those of the pagans whose gods were demons and impure spirits. Rabbi 'Aqiba, complaining of his own ill success in magic, said, "When a man fasts in order that an unclean spirit should rest on him, the pure spirit should do so. But what can I do since our iniquities are the cause of our difficulties? For it is said that your iniquities are dividing you from your God." The context leaves no doubt of the magical reference. But 'Aqiba is not, of course, represented in the Talmud as a magician, because that term was a term of abuse. The fact that a man was represented as a supernatural being is in itself a suspicious item, for this was a common claim of magicians and a regular result of magical operation. Thus there were those who, by study of the Torah, sought to master it so as to be able to use directly, for their own purposes, its creative and miraculous powers; in 'Aqiba's words, they "fasted that a pure spirit should rest upon them."

Such men could do miracles for and by themselves, not just ask to have them done for them. And this mastery and use of the Torah made Torah a source of magical, not merely supernatural, power. But again it must be stressed that rabbis never called themselves magicians. On the contrary, they consistently and explicitly disapproved of "magic." But many of the things they did, especially the supernatural character alleged to have been imparted to them by their knowledge of Torah, must be seen in the context of antiquity as appropriate to divine-men or magicians. Unique to the rabbis is the claim that their miracles, supernatural graces, and magical actions derived from the Torah rather than from some other source of supernatural power. To them, this was sufficient justification.

v. TORAH-POWER

The rabbis were believed to be able to pray more effectively than other people, the heads of schools most effectively of all. So it was said that "in the time of R. Joseph" (meaning, when he was the head of the school), there was a famine. The rabbis asked him to offer prayers for mercy. He replied, "If Elisha with whom, when the rabbis departed, there still remained two thousand and two hundred disciples, did not offer up prayers for mercy in a time of famine, should I . . . ?"

(b. Ket. 106a)

Further, only when R. Joseph became head of a school was he able to solve a certain legal problem. Rava said that Ahasuerus, the king mentioned in the Book of Esther, believed that the rabbis would protect Israel because they were careful to keep the commandments.

The basis of the belief in the exceptional powers of the rabbis lay in the anterior conviction that study of Torah and performance of the commandments produced heavenly favor, thus resulting in protection against evil (demons and Satan) and in special blessings:

R. Joseph said that doing a commandment protects [from suffering] and rescues [from evil inclination] when one is doing it, but afterwards, while it protects, it does not rescue.

Rava said that while one is engaged in study of Torah, the act of study protects and rescues, but otherwise, study of Torah protects but does not rescue. As to a commandment under all circumstances it protects but does not rescue.

(b. Soṭ. 21a)

Both Rava and Abaye said that sin could be expiated not through sacrifice, but through study of the Torah and good deeds. Although Rabbah and Abaye were supposedly descended from the house of Eli, they were able to overcome the ancient curse against that house through devotion to the Torah and, in Abaye's case, good deeds as well. Therefore, in spite of the fact that descendants of Eli were not supposed to live past the age of twenty, Rabbah was rewarded by a life of forty years, and Abaye, sixty years.

Study of Torah was a subject for comment when it did not yield exceptional prowess:

Rava said, "Is there any greatness in propounding problems? In the years of Rav Judah, their whole studies were confined to the laws of *Neziqin* [civil law and torts], while we study [much more . . .], yet Rav Judah [merely] took off his shoes and the rain came, while we cry out but are not heard [lit.: "no one pays attention to us"]. But [it is because] the Holy One blessed be He requires the heart . . ."

(b. Sanh. 106b)

R. Papa said to Abaye, "What is the difference between us and the ancients? For them, miracles were done, and for us, no miracles are done. If it is on account of learning, in the years of Rav Judah, they studied only *Neziqin,* and we study all six orders of the Mishnah, and when Rav Judah reached [a certain passage, he was perplexed by it, while we understand that same passage. But he could produce rain, and we cannot]."

Abaye replied to him, "The ancients gave their lives for the sanctification of God's name, but we do not do so."

(b. Ber. 20a)

Rabbah once decreed a fast. He prayed, but no rain came.

People thereupon remarked to him, "When Rav Judah ordained a fast, rain did fall."

He replied, "What can I do? Is it because of studies? We are superior to him, because in the time of Rav Judah . . . [as above]. Yet when Rav Judah removed one shoe . . . But when we cry out the whole day, no one hears us. Is it because of some deed? If so, let anyone who knows of it tell it. What can the great men of the generation do, however, when their generation does not seem good [warrant miracles]?"

(b. Ta. 24a-b)

The disciples of Rav Judah—Rava, Abaye, and Rabbah—preserved these three fundamentally different stories of how the several masters had uttered the same saying on the disparity of learning and miraculous power between their generation and the former one. Presumably, therefore, this saying must have been prior to the stories both in time and in importance, and clearly some intrinsic relationship between mastery of Torah and the ability to make rain was assumed. The masters did not deny this relationship. It was a disappointment to them that they could not do what the ancients—whose achievements in learning were less impressive than theirs—could easily accomplish. The articulated sense of disparity between intellectual achievement and theurgical power leaves no doubt that the former was expected to yield the latter.

The righteous were even believed to have the creative power of God, as is strikingly manifested in the following:

Rava said, "If a righteous man desires it, he can be a creator of a world for it is written, *But your iniquities have distinguished* . . . (Is. 59:2). [That is, but for sin, a man's power would equal that of God, and he could create a world.]

Rabbah created a man, and sent him to R. Zera. R. Zera spoke to him,

83

but he did not answer. He said to him, "You are a creature of the magicians [Zoroastrian Magi]. Return to your dust."

(b. Sanh. 65b)

Learning and piety thus reshape a man in the likeness of God, and therefore endow him with God's powers of creation. God had made the world through Torah, and masters of Torah could similarly do wonderful acts of creation. Rava said that only sin prevented man from performing miracles, like both Rabbah, who was able to create a man, and R. Zera, who was able to destroy one.

Although the rabbis could attain the creative power of God, this did not mean that they were "like God." The following story is an example of the limitations of a rabbi's extraordinary power:

Rabbah and R. Zera feasted together on Purim. They became drunk, and Rabbah arose and cut R. Zera's throat. The next day he prayed on his behalf and resurrected him.
Next year he asked, "Will your honor come and feast with me?"
He replied, "A miracle does not always happen."

(b. Meg. 7b)

The rabbi was able to persuade God to resurrect the dead. However, had Rabbah been "like God," R. Zera would have had no legitimate reason to refuse a second invitation. The refusal given indicated that the miracle was accomplished not strictly by magic but through prayer and as a rather uncertain reward for merits. God could effect miracles without assistance; the rabbi generally had to rely upon prayer or merits. That is the difference between this story, an ordinary one of prayer and its reward, and those in which the rabbis' own extraordinary powers (probably acquired by prayer, study, or other merits) were usable directly and uncontingently.

If knowledge of the Torah yielded magic, magic could also be used to produce greater mastery of the Torah. Abaye believed that a certain bird, properly eaten, would help one increase in wisdom. Half the right side and half the left were to be eaten and the remainder placed in a brass tube. The tube was sealed with sixty sealings and suspended on one's arm. After studying as much as desired, the would-be scholar had to consume the other half of the bird, thus sealing in the new learning. If he failed to eat the other half, he would forget what he had learned.

This faith in the worldly benefits of studying the Torah, keeping the commandments, and acting virtuously was not the invention of the rabbis. From biblical times, it had been believed that if the Israelites faithfully kept the covenant and the commandments, they would enjoy prosperity. Such was the theory of Deuteronomy. The rabbis simply arrogated to themselves and their activities promises that were earlier believed to depend upon the good works of priests, prophets, and other holy men and upon popular adherence to their teachings. Thus theurgical skills were regarded as an authentication —although not the only one—of the fact that rabbis were holy men, or saints, or righteous.

The saying that only sin prevented men from doing the things God could do may be reversed. For example, if Rabbah could create a man, then obviously he must be sinless, a master of great learning and merits. His theurgical ability testified to his pure, sinless condition as a master of Torah. That is not to suggest that repeating words of Torah was an incantation of the same substance as saying an anti-demonic formula. But if repeating words of Torah could prevent the angel of death from approaching Rabbah, then repeating words of Torah did serve on occasion as an incantation.

Although great learning in Torah did not lead *only* or invariably to the ability to do such wonders as making men, cows, or rain, the ascription of supernatural power must nevertheless be seen as a primary attribute of leading masters in the schools. It is the attribute which most closely paralleled those of the "divine-man" of antiquity —a man believed to embody divine power and virtue—for the unity of faith, wisdom, and unusual ability was everywhere taken for granted. "Knowing" and "doing" were in no way separable; the rabbi's "wisdom" derived from Torah, and so did his supernatural, or magical, skills. To no one in antiquity could such a conception have been alien.

Jews were famed for the excellence of their magic, as shown in Acts 19:11-20. To the extent that magicians were considered disreputable, no faithful community would regard its holy men as magicians. But where magic was an expected and normal trait of religious virtuosi, everyone supposed that the holy men of the community could produce magic. What was "Torah" or perhaps "white magic" to Jews may have been witchcraft or black magic to gentile neighbors, and vice versa. It was a subjective distinction at best. For Jews, the rabbi as living Torah was surely as close as one could possibly come to the revealed, or incarnate, god of other religious groups.

A striking portrait of the wisdom of Solomon as drawn by Josephus should be noted:

There was no form of nature with which he [Solomon] was not acquainted or which he passed over without examining, but he studied them all philosophically and revealed the most complete knowledge of their several properties. And God granted him knowledge of the art used against demons for the benefit and healing of men. He also composed incantations by which illnesses are relieved, and left behind forms of exorcisms with which those possessed by demons drive them out, never to return. And this kind of cure is of very great power among us to this day.

> (Josephus, *Jewish Antiquities*, VIII,
> 44-45, trans H. Thackeray, V, 595)

Healing arts, exorcisms, incantations—these all testified to the grace of God no less than did mastery of Torah or other forms of saintliness. The rabbis took pride in their theurgical attainments, which, they said, were made possible by Torah.

vi. STUDY OF TORAH

Study of Torah was just that: primarily an intellectual enterprise whose supernatural effects were decidedly secondary. The resources of the schools were knowledge of the laws and traditions that for the rabbis constituted the Torah of Moses.

The actual method of learning used by the academies had nothing whatever to do with magic. The "Torah" of the rabbis was essentially no more than a legal tradition which had to be studied by the classical legal methods. The rabbis were expected to act as did other holy men, but they themselves respected legal learning and the capacity to reason about cases. Not everyone would achieve such skills of reasoning any more than everyone could make rain, and the academies doubtless attracted many who could only memorize and repeat what they knew. The whole process of learning and not merely its creative and innovative aspects, however, was regarded as sacred, for the words themselves were holy.

The following exposition from the school of R. 'Anan exemplifies this process:

What is the meaning of the Scripture, *You that ride on white asses, that sit on rich cloths, and that walk by the way, tell of it* (Judges 5:10).

Those that *ride on asses* are the sages who go from city to city and from province to province to study Torah.

*White*—means that they make it clear as the noon hour.

*Sitting on cloths*—means that they judge a case truly.

*And that walk*—refers to masters of Scripture.

*On the way*—these are masters of Mishnah.

*Tell of it*—refers to masters of Talmud, all of whose conversation concerns matters of Torah.

(b. Eruv. 54b)

Found in the Song of Deborah, this verse about the victory of Israel over the Canaanites was explained by the rabbis as a description of the triumph of the Lord in the "wars of the Torah," a frequent image of rabbinical Judaism, and the consequent celebration by the people of the Lord. That people included many whose talents were limited, but who, added all together, constituted, and celebrated, the Lord's triumph. Some, like itinerant philosophers, would wander in search of teachings. Others had a great skill at clarification. Others were able and selfless judges. Still others merely knew Scripture, or Mishnah, or Talmud, but spoke of nothing else. Here is the integrated, mature vision of the academies: a whole people devoted to Revelation, each in his way and according to his talent.

Mere knowledge of the traditions, however, was held in contempt unless it was accompanied by personal charisma of some kind, whether expressed through brilliance of reasoning or unusual powers of another sort. It was not only what one knew that mattered, but also what he could do with what he knew, whether his actions were narrowly magical, or parabolic in quality. "The Tanna [professional memorizer of traditions] repeats and does not know what he is saying, the Magus mumbles and does not know what he is saying," so went a proverb quoted by a fourth-century rabbi. The Tanna of the Babylonian academy who had memorized the Tannaitic [Mishnah] traditions of the academy was not a figure who won broad public admiration. All those who did were noteworthy for their miracles, or for their public action as judges and administrators, or for their insight as logicians, or for their medical and astrological learning, or for their knowledge of Scripture and its contemporary meaning. These were *rabbis*. The rest were mere bystanders, regardless of the usefulness of their learning.

87

## vii. Rabbinic Theology

Rabbinic theology included two important elements. First were secret doctrines pertaining to the being and essence of God, the mysteries of history and redemption, and the like. These doctrines were studied in the schools and rarely, if ever, taught or even alluded to outside of them. Second, the rabbis publicly offered a self-consistent and comprehensive view of man's relationship to God. Man had to submit to God's will, and he demonstrated his submission through observing the commandments. If he sinned by not doing so, he would be held responsible. Punishment would follow in this world through suffering, but the suffering had to be gladly accepted, for it insured that one had at least begun atonement here, and hence could worry less about the world to come. If people sinned and nonetheless prospered, or if they did not sin and yet suffered, an easy explanation was available. The wicked might enjoy this world, but in time to come they would pay a terrible penalty. Similarly the righteous might suffer now, but in time to come they would enjoy a great reward. This neat account sufficed for the orderly conceptions of the schools, although probably not for the disorderly life of the streets.

Other elements of rabbinic theology cannot be ignored. Demons; witchcraft and incantations; revelations through omens, dreams, and astrology; the efficacy of prayers and magical formulas; rabbinical blessings and curses; the merit acquired through study of the Torah and obedience to both the commandments and the sages—all these constituted important components of the rabbinic world-view. A comprehensive account of the rabbis' beliefs about this world and those above and below and about the invisible beings that populated space and carried out divine orders would yield a considerably more complicated theology than that briefly given here. Its main outlines, however, would not be much modified, for magic, angels, demons, and the rest represented the way the rabbis thought matters worked themselves out—all these elements constituted the *technology* of the rabbis' theological world-view.

The spiritual attitude of both rabbis and the masses could be described in the following way: "We are absolutely worthless, and are now deprived even of the former ways of finding favor with You. Once there was a Temple, and we could offer sacrifice there, but now it is no more, so we must give the sacrifice of our flesh and blood.

But who are we to propitiate, we who are of no consequence and have no future? We are nothing, except that we are *Israel,* the children of men you loved, and bearers of the revelation you delivered.

"Even in the most private moments of life, we are not alone, but are surrounded by the merits of the fathers and the presence of memories of the sacred moments of our history. Nor are we hopeless, because we look forward to the fulfillment of the promises made to the prophets in olden times. We are sanctified in all which we do out of love and loyalty to you. In the hour of our greatest private joy, at the marriage canopy, we remember both the public sorrow and the coming joy of Zion, and recall not only its destruction, but what was said by Jeremiah when it was destroyed, that it *will* be rebuilt.

"So if we are sinners, we lie in the hands of a God of great mercy. The passage of the seasons, which we witness regularly month by month, testifies to your enduring sovereignty. Just as the moon keeps your laws, so do we, and just as it testifies to the greatness of its maker, so would we. When we find ourselves in a time of danger, we turn to you and beseech your blessing."

The ordinary people would have comprehended and believed in the faith of the rabbis as it is here expressed. While the prayers concerning study of the Torah and the discussions of proper procedures in the academies or of benedictions may not have been understood by the people, the spiritual situation revealed in the rabbis' prayers was precisely congruent to theirs. They too were "Israel," and they revered the Scriptures and remembered its lessons. They too longed for the coming of the Messiah, and although unable to express their yearnings in the evocative and noble language of the rabbis, they surely could have adopted the rabbinical liturgies without any difficulty.

The more narrowly academic concerns included the precise and detailed discussions of laws on how and when to pray, the proper blessings to say over one thing or another, the conditions for interrupting prayer, and the like. It is doubtful that ordinary people were much bothered by liturgical issues posed to the masters or that the instruction imparted to the disciples reached a broad audience. To learn the proper way of saying grace proved terribly difficult even for many students, and outsiders could scarcely have comprehended all the rules. Indeed, knowing and keeping these rules was one of the important significations that a person had entered the rabbinical state. Yet one must not suppose that the issues of the common faith were divorced from the rabbinical discussions, or that the legalistic rabbis really had no very vivid spiritual life. The prayers they composed testify to the contrary, and so does the seriousness with which they considered the whole matter of prayer. It was precisely *because* they believed in prayer as fervently as did ordinary people that they thought one should pray with at least the decorum and respect shown to an earthly king of kings; therefore, they seriously inquired into the proper and improper procedures for praying. In this sense, the rabbis' laws do represent the continuation of popular faith: if the people believed that prayer mattered, then the rabbis—who were, after all, lawyers—set out the rules of conduct and procedure which would conform to such a belief.

Prayers composed by rabbis centered upon four major themes: (1) the Temple and its cult, (2) the wrath of God, which was revealed in an hour of crisis, (3) the humility and helplessness of man, and (4) the corpus of ideas and symbols embodied in the sacred history of Israel. Above all, however, one is struck by the intensity of rabbinical prayers concerning the Messianic kingdom. In the liturgy for the marriage ceremony, the center of attention focused upon the coming joy of Zion, which was prefigured by the delight of bridegroom and bride. Just as one loved the other, and rejoiced in that love, so in time would God again espouse Israel in Zion, and rejoice in her. The private joy of life was thus seen to be paradigmatic for the public event of coming history. It was the Messianic hope which became vivid in times of difficulty. The deep and abiding longing for the Messiah's coming characterized master, disciple, and outsider alike. Although they might accommodate themselves to the conditions of the current life, the Jews saw this world as merely transitory and impoverished. In time to come the advent of the true and permanent age would inaugurate an age of fulfillment and completion. Although the prayers and discussions of the rabbis seem private, personal, and ahistorical, they must be seen against the broader framework of faith in which they found meaning. Within the humble affairs of Israel's life at that time, one might discern, though darkly, the shadowed reflections of the great illumination that was to come. Both in and for that light, Jews prayed.

viii.  THE RITUALS OF "BEING A RABBI"

Despite common elements of a faith shared with the masses, the rabbis' stress on Torah led to the development of customs, rites,

90

and practices unique to the rabbinical estate, thus setting that estate apart as one enjoying special privileges and bearing special responsibilities. Following is a story illustrating the ways in which rabbinic language and etiquette proved highly formalized:

A certain man from Nehardea came to a butcher shop in Pumbedita. He said to them, "Give me meat."

They said to him, "Wait until the attendant of Rav Judah b. Yeḥezqel takes, and then we shall serve you."

He said, "Who is this Judah b. *Shevisqel* who comes before me to take precedence?"

They went and told Rav Judah.

He excommunicated him.

They said, "The man from Nehardea is accustomed to call people slaves."

Rav Judah pronounced the man a slave.

The man went and called him [Rav Judah] to court before R. Naḥman [the appellate authority, to appeal Judah's decision].

When a summons was brought, Rav Judah came before R. Huna [to ask the advice of a friend on whether to respond to the summons].

Rav Judah said to him, "Should I go or not?" Huna said, "You do not have to go, because you are an important man, but on account of the honor of the house of the *Nasi* [exilarch], rise and go."

He came and found R. Naḥman making a rail. He said, "Do you not agree with the teaching of R. Huna b. Idi in the name of Samuel, 'Once a man is appointed administrator over the community, he is prohibited to work before three men.' "

R. Naḥman said, "I am only making a portion of a *gundrita* [rail]."

Rav Judah replied, "Is *ma'akah* [rail] unacceptable, as is written in Revelation, or *meḥizah* [rail] as the rabbis call it?"

R. Naḥman said to him, "Will the master sit on a *karpita* [chair]?"

Rav Judah said, "And is *safsal* [chair], as the rabbis say, or *'iẓtaba,* as people say, unacceptable?"

R. Naḥman said to him, "Will the master eat *'etronga?*"

Rav Judah replied, "Thus did Samuel say, 'Whoever says *'etronga* is one-third puffed up?' Either one should say *'etrog,* as the rabbis call it, or *'etroga,* as the people say."

"Will the master drink *'anbaga?*"

"He said to him, "Is *'ispargus,* as the rabbis say, or *'anpak* as the people say, unacceptable?"

R. Naḥman said, "Shall my daughter Donag bring something to drink?"

Rav Judah said to him, "So said Samuel, 'One must not make use of a woman.' "

"She is a minor."

"Explicitly did Samuel state, 'One may make use of no woman whatsoever, whether adult or minor.' "

"Will you send a greeting to my wife Yalta?"

Rav Judah said to him, "So said Samuel, 'Even the voice of a woman is erotic.' "

"Through her husband?!"

"So said Samuel," he replied, " 'One must not inquire after the welfare of a woman by any means.' "

(b. Qid. 70a-b)

In this story the imposition of particular, rabbinical conventions—Torah-traditions—upon a perfectly routine and ordinary encounter is striking. Knowledge of those traditions would have been demonstrated even by words people used for ordinary objects and by how one greeted one's fellowman. These may be seen as instances of in-group rites; other rites would include the wearing of characteristic garments, the saying of prayers not said by ordinary people, the way in which one related to one's own master, sexual practices, and peculiarly rabbinic rituals pertaining to every other aspect of daily life.

The rabbis held that study of the Torah had to lead to a reformation of the disciple's entire way of living so that even the masses would be able readily to recognize the man as a disciple. Deportment testified to the status of a man at least as authoritatively as did his ability to quote rabbinic traditions. Entry into the rabbinical estate was not attained through birth, although some rabbis were the children of masters of the early generations. It was not reached through social or economic status, for disciples came from the poor classes and only the heads of schools consistently achieved great wealth. Political preference did not help, for the exilarch could not appoint ordinary people to the rabbinate, but had to accept the qualifications first achieved and recognized in the schools. One entered the rabbinical estate through a combination of learning and imitation of the rabbis, resulting in the acquisition of clear-cut patterns of behavior and personal bearing which thus became signs of membership. To be a disciple represented a highly ritualistic and formalized way of living, a way in which one's manner of speaking, eating, walking, and (of greatest consequence) conduct with certain other similarly designated figures took on religious consequence.

Why did the rabbis stress the significance of rabbinical deportment-rituals? If the ordinary people were expected to obey the rabbi and copy his patterns of behavior, then they had to be able to immediately recognize that he was a holy man and unlike themselves, was obedient to supernatural disciplines. Just as the Christian monks and nuns achieved holy status by their exceptional asceticism, which often led to sacred vagrancy, so did the rabbis by their constant repetition of words of Torah, by their extraordinary deference to their masters, by their speech, clothing, way of walking, behavior with women, and the like. This strange, awesome, and holy behavior, which set the rabbi apart and attested to his singular character, was, therefore, an important source of his influence over the ordinary people.

It would be a gross error, however, to overestimate the differences separating the way of life of the ordinary Jews from that of the rabbinical estate. Jewish Babylonia knew the distinction between layman and rabbi, but that distinction was not invariably critical. In general the rabbis' merely conventional social manners or customs were deepened into spiritual conceptions and magnified by deeply mythic ways of thinking. In the villages the ordinary people regarded the rabbi as another holy and therefore exceptional man, but still as a man heart and soul at one in community with other Jews. The rabbinical ideal was anti-dualistic; the rabbis believed that all Israel, not just saints, prophets, and sages, stood at Sinai and bore common responsibilities. No one conceived of two ways of living a holy life—two virtues or two salvations—but of only one Torah to be studied and observed by all, and thus the cutting edge of rabbinical separateness was blunted.

The inevitable gap between the holy man and the layman was further reduced by the deep concern felt by rabbis for the conduct of the masses. This concern led them to involve themselves in the everyday affairs of ordinary people, and it produced considerable impact upon daily life.

A review of the primary distinctive characteristics of the rabbinical school will show that the rabbis could not have created unscalable walls of social or religious difference. The sages spent a good part of their years in these schools; ordinary Jews obviously did not. Yet the schools were not monasteries. Disciples who left but who remained loyal to the school's way of life did not engage in ascetic disciplines of an outlandish sort, calculated to utterly divide the sages' way of living from that of normal men. They married. They ate regularly and chose edible food, not wormwood or locusts or refuse. They lived in villages, not in the wilderness. They did not make their livelihood through holy vagrancy. Their clothes were not supposed to be tattered or in rags. These differences between rabbis and other types of holy men, such as the Christian monks and the Manichaean elect, are obvious and therefore all the more important. The sages sought the society of ordinary Jews, so they lived in the villages rather than in the countryside ("wilderness"). Not engaged in begging ("holy vagrancy"), they owned property and were glad of it. They occupied important and permanent positions in the administration of communal life, and so came into constant and intimate contact with the common people. Access to the rabbinical schools remained open to all, and the rabbis actively proselytized within the community to gain new candidates for their schools. Advantages of birth were minimal. In no way did the rabbis form a caste or a clan; the right marriage counted for little.

What, therefore, did the peculiarities of the rabbinical way of living amount to? A rabbi could eat with any other Jew in Babylonia because the biblical taboos about food were widely observed. The differences between the rabbis' interpretation of the taboos and those advanced by others diminished, as in time the rabbis' growing domination made their unique exegeses seem more commonplace. For example, although the rabbis said grace at meals and offered intelligible blessings of food, they were willing to teach others just what those blessings and prayers meant. Nothing in the rabbinical ritual of eating was to be kept secret. A person showed himself "ignorant" if he violated the rituals. His remedy was to go to a sage to study and learn, and this was explicitly recommended by the rabbis.

The rabbis had their own words for various objects, and knowing these words was a sign of membership in the rabbinical estate. Yet the rabbis spoke the language of the people not only when among them but also in the schools. There is no evidence that the language of the schools was Hebrew instead of Aramaic, although fixed *forms* in Hebrew were creatively used. In any event, apart from the usual difficulties of dialect and local custom, any rabbi could communicate with any outsider, and, what is more important, rabbis made no effort to formulate a secret, private language for themselves, but only a distinctive vocabulary considered appropriate to their scholastic

94

and social status. They clearly regarded their speech as "more cultivated" and as evidence of better education. But this did not render their language alien to the community at large. It merely signified that a person was part of the in-group and therefore had to be all the more comprehensible to outsiders. Eating, clothing, speech—these everyday matters—revealed both particularities and commonalities, but overall these differences did not amount to much.

Only two really substantially differentiating characteristics were observable. First was the relationship between master and disciple. The rabbis' social life followed forms wholly alien to those of outsiders. The disciple revered the master as a living Torah and humbled himself before him as before God. The outsider honored the master as a learned man, fantasized about his magical powers, submitted to his judicial authority, and accepted his communal influence. These reflected basically different attitudes: on one hand stood a living myth; on the other, the superficial effects of that myth. Furthermore, the disciple of the sages conformed to personality traits and behavior patterns which would have been quite unnatural for ordinary folk. He forced himself into a posture of abject humility with implications far beyond what outsiders could have comprehended or accepted. His reverence for the master was only a little lower than his fear of the Lord. His imitation of the master's deeds and his preservation of the memory of those deeds shaped a religious discipline quite alien to the workaday life of common people. The humility shown to God and to the master was supposed to extend to the disciple's behavior with everyone else.

The personality traits appropriate to such piety had to be extended from heaven to earth. Historical events and moral virtues not only corresponded to one another but actually came into contact in the formation of the sage's personality. The honor paid by a disciple to his master and the close imitation of his actions consequently constituted the most striking distinction between the social life of the rabbi and that of the outsider. The service of the disciple to the master was required of the disciple but of no one else, and a particular disciple served a particular master, not a whole coterie of authorities. A highly exceptional relationship was therefore formed. One who had studied merely Scriptures, and even Mishnah, remained a boor, learned but no different from a Magus, unless he had also "served" a master through imitation of the master's *way*, subjecting himself to his discipline and that of the schools.

The second characteristic separating rabbis from common Jews was study. Obviously the reasons were not that ordinary people did not understand the need for information, that they were entirely ignorant of the world and its way, or that they knew nothing of traditions. The people knew the Scriptures. They listened to the reading of the Torah in the synagogues. Prophetic writings and, for a long time, passages of wisdom literature were also regularly read to them. The masses observed the Sabbath, the festivals, the holy days, and food and sex taboos. All these observances required knowledge, and the constant exposure to Scriptures and to the sages produced a considerable amount of it. Therefore, the "learning" of the rabbis cannot be spoken of in total contrast to the "ignorance" of the masses. Unless there is an acceptance of the rabbinical belief in their sole possession of the oral Torah, the people cannot be regarded as "ignorant" at all.

What the average Jews ordinarily did not know and the rabbis always did know was the one thing that made a common man into a rabbi: *"Torah" learned through discipleship.* It begs the question to speak of the ordinary people as "ignorant of Judaism." One does not have to exaggerate the educational attainments of the community as a whole to recognize that learning in the rabbinical traditions did not by itself separate the rabbi from other people. What was important was the rabbi's attitude toward his *own* study. Extrinsic qualities deriving from the mythic context transformed the natural actions of learning facts or ideas or memorizing sayings— which anyone might have done—into the ritual actions unique to the rabbi.

What actually happened in the rabbinical school? First, masters and disciples gathered together, and the master taught the traditions of Torah. These were encapsulated in formulas, and the student memorized the exact words, not merely the sense, of those traditions. Second, the schoolmaster frequently served as a community authority, a judge and administrator, so the disciple would follow the master as he did his business, keeping in mind the ways in which the master applied the law to specific cases. It is difficult to say whether the schools met in buildings devoted to that purpose, although it appears that they did. The disciples would come to the town where the masters had assembled, and there they would live for many years. Outside of the towns in which schools were located,

96

however, the rabbis could not have constituted a significant proportion of the Jewish population.

The *way* of the schools was to become *law* for the community at a future time, but for the period covered in this study, the separateness of the rabbinical estate persisted and produced its own worldly effects. The rabbi was endowed both in his own mind and in the practical life of society with a glorious reward. Insight into the joy he felt in his life can be derived from Rabina's saying that the rabbis, "those who love God," shall be "as the sun when he goes forth in his might." Through Torah they did not overcome natural death, but they did find serenity and strength in the conviction that Torah and commandments shielded them in this world and promised the blessings of the world to come. The rabbis saw themselves as the intermediaries between heaven and earth, the new priests able to offer sacrifice more pleasing to heaven than the earlier burnt-offerings. They believed that through Torah they would be able to bring about the restoration of the ancient Temple and the establishment of the Messianic kingdom of God. For such achievements the reward of a measure of worldly honor was little enough. The respect of ordinary Jews for the rabbis, and of the sages for one another, quite naturally corresponded to the sages' view of cosmic realities. The glory of the world to come would prove commensurate, for the sage would feast in the splendor of the *Shekhinah*, God's presence on earth.

The "Judaism" of the rabbis at this time was in no degree normative, and speaking descriptively, the schools could not be called "elite." Whatever their aspirations for the future and pretensions in the present, the rabbis, though powerful and influential, constituted a minority group seeking to exercise authority without much governmental support, to dominate without substantial means of coercion. What they wanted to accomplish was the formation of the kingdom of priests and holy people demanded at Sinai, and to do so according to the revelation of Sinai as they alone possessed it. Admittedly a description of the rabbinical schools is hardly a portrait of the religious life of Babylonian Jewry. Yet, in the author's view, the rabbis did more and more set the standard, the golden measure, the royal way.

# Chapter Four

# Function

## i. Power, Myth, and Function

The institutional sources of power within Judaism and the mythic explanations of power wielded by those institutions cannot be readily distinguished. A consideration of the exilarch, whose political power derived from the Iranian state, required an investigation into how he explained to the Jews his rule over the Jewish group. That explanation had nothing to do with Iranian politics; its outlines revealed an essentially Messianic story. Similarly, a survey of the Torah-myth of the rabbis caused an appraisal of its political implications for the structure of power within the community, although that myth is essentially a supernatural and religious, not political, story. Further, a study of the Torah-myth, institutions, and the social estate that embodied the myth could not ignore implications for the exercise of social control—power—within the Jewish community. The rabbis' beliefs led them to want to affect peoples' behavior. That aspiration forced them to seek access to the centers of power within Jewry. One therefore cannot overlook the interrelationships of power and myth. These interrelationships are most fully revealed in the functioning of rabbinic Judaism in the everyday life of Babylonian Jewry.

Examples of actual rabbinical use of power all pertain to minor details of daily affairs, unimportant particularities. The real change —the transformation of the ancient Judaism of Babylonia to conform to the rabbinic belief in the "whole Torah of Moses," that is, the "rabbinization" of Babylonian Jewry—is nowhere described in presently available sources. At the beginning of the period under study, the "whole Torah" characterized a small and unimportant group of men; by the end, it was fully realized by the major centers of Babylonian Jewish life. The process of social change that must have taken place is discernible only through a few glimpses into seemingly static situations. And these glimpses tell of trivialities.

Evidently the great social issues were debated and settled through a focus on inconsequential matters. A nineteenth-century example of this can be seen in the debates on the reformation of Judaism. These debates, which occurred in Germany and America, were represented by all participants as relating to such comparative trivialities as whether one may pray in German rather than in Hebrew, or whether men and women may sit together in the synagogue rather than by themselves as formerly, or whether instrumental music may be permitted in synagogue services. Only later was the real issue under debate clearly stated: Would Judaism accept the norms, social-religious conventions, and values of the modern West, or would it persist in its own way as it always had, separate and aloof from those values? And behind that issue lay a still less openly articulated question: Would the Jew become like everyone else except with respect to his religious beliefs, or would he remain, as he had for many centuries, essentially a resident alien? For all parties to the debate, these issues were settled before they were ever explicitly faced and argued.

An understanding of the distinction between political *power* and religious *influence* is essential to a discussion of the bases of rabbinical leadership over the ordinary people. If a rabbi could resort to court punishments, such as the ban or the lash, or forcibly require a defendant to accept the court judgment in a case of property litigation, or impose fines, then it may be said that he had concrete, coercive, political *power* to carry out the law. However, another sort of power was that wielded by the rabbi over people who believed he could curse or bless them with actual, measurable results, or who thought he was a holy man, able to bring down the favor or wrath of an ever-interested Divinity and his legions of angels and demons, or who accepted his claim to know just what God wanted of Israel in this particular place and time. That power was no less "coercive" in its way than was police power in its several forms. It

99

is referred to as "religious *influence*" to distinguish between what the rabbis could do as agents of the Jewish government and what they could do as holy men.

As agents of the Jewish government, the rabbis decided according to rabbinical law any cases involving personal status and transfers of property. A few other types could be adjudicated by their courts as well, but these two were the chief categories of law which rabbinical courts enforced with Iranian and exilarchic support. As holy men, the rabbis exerted religious influence in a most concrete sense. Their religious influence probably was not in the sense that the appeal of an individual rabbi's personality affected or moved ordinary people. Some of the rabbis did exhibit striking personalities, but that had little to do with the response of the people to their orders. It was religion or magic and not personal charisma which influenced the workaday world. People were either so frightened of the evil the rabbis could bring down upon them, or so eager for blessings they could promise in this world and in the next, or so impressed by their mastery of supposedly ancient teachings which God had revealed at Mount Sinai, that they submitted to the rabbis. Whether this submission was against their own will or otherwise hardly matters; they were subjected, or subjected themselves, to the "spiritual power" of the rabbis. That spiritual power was not divorced from material matters. On the contrary, it is quite clear that a curse was believed to be practically effective over crops or commerce; a blessing would generate male children or open the gates of heaven.

The only useful distinction between "power" and "influence" must be located in the basis of coercion. When the rabbi could rely on the exilarch to see to it that a court order was obeyed, he exerted political power; when he had to resort to the curse or ban, he used religious influence. Thus, rabbinical *power,* deriving from the authority and ultimate support of Iranian government and functioning through the exilarchate, effected the widespread enforcement of civil laws. It applied to extraordinary matters such as contested divorces or marriage contracts, broken contracts, disputed property and real estate, torts, and similar occurrences. On the other hand, supernatural rabbinical *influence* pertained to ordinary life, to the conduct of normal people in everyday circumstances, as well as to matters of faith, cult, rite, and taboo beyond court jurisdiction.

It would be a mistake, however, to suppose that these forms of coercion ever were completely distinguished from one another. The judge in court, able to order lashes or excommunication, could also curse the guilty party or cast an evil eye. Furthermore, the administrator of community affairs, who dealt with matters which, by their nature, could hardly be brought to court, and who in general was able to exert his will through influence rather than political coercion, normally was also the court-judge who might try a civil case involving the same recalcitrant. The sinner was a criminal, and vice versa. And the rabbinical judge-administrator was always the holy man who knew the Torah, whose clothing, speech, and conduct set him apart from other Jews. The rabbi as an extraordinary, holy man achieved his greatest effect in commonplace and ongoing daily life. The rabbi as lawyer, judge, and administrator, carrying out fundamentally routine, political tasks, was related to the exceptional events which resulted in court cases.

## ii. RABBINICAL AUTHORITY

As discussed in Chapter Three, the rabbis did not rule as a privileged caste. The rabbinate did not constitute an economic class, or occupy a single stratum within Jewish society. While many of the most important rabbis emerged from, or became part of, the upper classes, their values or ideals were not intrinsically upper-class. They recognized tensions between themselves and the rich and powerful classes. They greatly encouraged the education of poor students. They were not a clerical group. They played no role in the liturgical or sacerdotal life of the Jewish community, nor did the synagogue afford them a special platform for their ideas, except when they spoke there. In Palestine they contended for power in earlier times with the priesthood, which did form a sacerdotal caste, but by the time under study the priests were no longer a significant or influential group within Babylonian Jewry, having long since accommodated themselves to a perfunctory and inconsequential place in ritual life alone. It is not even certain that they continued to receive priestly offerings.

The rabbis' claim against those of the sons of Aaron (the priests) and the seed of David (the exilarch) was not based solely upon learning in the law or Scriptures. Had they depended only upon their possession of learning alone, the generally acknowledged superior genealogy of priest and Davidide alike in a community obsessed with genealogy would have proved insurmountable. The

101

priests had earlier had their own legal traditions, and those traditions still were believed by numerous Jews to be the proper guide to the application of revelation to the current age. Before A.D. 70, a priestly court based in the Jerusalem Temple had existed to issue *ad hoc* decrees as needed. In addition, the exilarch proved quite able to hire bureaucrats and judges, lawyers who were not rabbis. Since none—not even rabbis—doubted that he had the most distinguished ancestry of all, the claim to superior learning alone could have meant little in the political economy of Babylonia.

At this point the *functional* importance of rabbinical magical power becomes apparent. The rabbi presented himself as, and was widely believed to be, a holy man whose merit and magic weighed at least as heavily as his learning, and whose learning encompassed far more than a collection of ancient traditions of scriptural exegesis. What was extraordinary about him was his mastery of a body of theurgical learning, the power of which rendered him exceptionally influential in both heaven and earth. His "Torah" included more than just the Scriptures revealed at Sinai or to the prophets, plus the accompanying oral traditions. If rabbinical knowledge, or gnosis, was an effective basis for public activities, it was because the rabbis could authenticate that knowledge by a wide variety of impressive proofs. No phenomenon above or below proved too hard for their understanding. Their wisdom was such that they could interpret natural phenomena and consort with heavenly beings. They were not physicians, but did possess sound knowledge about healing. The substance and effects of their gnosis sufficiently impressed other Jews that they were seen to have been transformed, by virtue of what they *knew,* into extraordinary men. Genealogy and politics could scarcely contend against "Torah"; but one must stress, it was Torah based as much upon holiness as upon knowledge of facts, even of mysteries, that characterized the rabbinical estate.

According to the rabbinic tradition, prophecy was suspended at the time of the prophet Malachi. However, Elijah continued to make his appearances to the rabbis. For example, R. 'Anan, a fourth-century master, supposedly received frequent visits from Elijah, who was teaching him. These supernatural appearances were not merely occasional or for brief instruction; they affected legal as much as theological discussions. Elijah communicated good advice to various other rabbis. The following is representative:

Said Elijah to Rav Judah brother of R. Sala the Pious, "Fall not into a passion and you will not sin. Drink not to excess and you will not sin. When you go forth on a journey, seek counsel of your Maker and go forth."

(b. Ber. 29b)

This story is one of a great many which depicted the teachings of Elijah to a rabbi. How is it to be understood? If the masses widely believed that the rabbis' teachings derived from a heavenly source, then rabbinical influence would have substantially exceeded what would otherwise have been accorded to them. Therefore, it is doubtful that the rabbis themselves would have discouraged this belief. On the other hand, there are no apparent grounds to suppose that Elijah-encounters were deliberate fabrications. What must have happened in such incidents is that a rabbi—living in a world in which people normally thought that demons or angels, including Elijah, frequently appeared to men—interpreted an unusual encounter in the light of quite natural expectations.

Rabbinic law does not convey a complete picture of daily affairs. Actions and conduct contrary to rabbinic dicta were commonplace. The two great bodies of archaeological evidence provide striking examples. First, no rabbinic source would have suggested the prediction of the existence of a synagogue wall such as was unearthed at Dura-Europos; nor is there very adequate assistance in rabbinic literature in interpreting the art of that synagogue. Second, the incantation texts from Nippur tell considerably more about the attitudes of the common people than does the Talmud, and what they tell is that the people had no hesitation whatever about making use of the best magical science of their day in achieving their life's purposes, an action which would have opposed rabbinical teachings.

To really have a true picture of everyday life, therefore, one must critically examine rabbinical sermons and sayings. For example, if one were to judge by sermons, there were Jews who did not obey the dietary laws, attend ritual baths, and otherwise comport themselves properly; and the rabbis had to call down upon their heads the most severe calamities by way of exhortation. It is even likely that there were Jews living in Babylonia who did not respect the rabbis, for Rav defined an *"Apikoros,"* or heretic (destined to be denied the blessings of the world to come) as one who insults a scholar (b. Sanh. 99b).

Taking a very realistic view of their contemporaries, the rabbis preached sermons that they must have felt necessary to encourage their people to behave in a moral manner, as illustrated in the following:

Rav said, "On account of four things is the property of householders confiscated by the state treasury: On account of those who defer payment of the labourer's hire; on account of those who withhold the hired laborer's wages; on account of those who remove the yoke from off their necks and place it on the necks of their fellows and on account of arrogance. And the sin of arrogance is equivalent to all the others, whereas of the humble it is written [Ps. 37:11], *But the humble shall inherit the land and delight themselves in the abundance of peace."*

(b. Suk. 29b)

R. Amram in the name of Rav said, "Three transgressions which no man escapes for a single day are sinful thought, calculation on prayer, and slander."

R. Judah in the name of Rav said, "Most people are guilty of robbery, a minority of lewdness, and all of slander."

(b. B.B. 164b)

If the following rabbinical source were taken as probative, one should have to conclude that the Jews did not fight on the Sabbath:

R. Judah in the name of Rav said, "If foreigners besiege Israelite towns, it is not permitted to sally forth against them, or to desecrate the Sabbath in any other way on their account, and so a Tanna taught as well."

(b. Eruv. 45a)

However, in fact, the Jewish state of Anilai and Asinai did conduct war on the Sabbath, not merely to overcome a siege, but to mount aggressive attacks on the enemy. Obviously a knowledge of the law's requirements does not reveal the actual behavior of the people.

Similarly, the rabbis' comments on the mores of their contemporaries present a picture quite at variance from the one which would be derived from strictly legal sources. An example:

R. Giddal in the name of Rav said, "If an inhabitant of Naresh kisses you, then count your teeth. If a man of Nehar Peḳod accompanies you, then it is because of the fine garments he sees on you. If a Pumbeditan accompanies you, change your lodging."

(b. Ḥul. 127a)

104

The rabbis laid great stress upon proper genealogies, holding that the descendants of illegitimate unions might not marry Jews. Babylonian rabbis insisted that Babylonia was, from the genealogical viewpoint, the acme of purity because Ezra had taken up with him all the unsuitable families. Moreover, they regarded ethical and social conduct as a suitable measure of genealogical purity:

Rav said, "Peace in Babylonia is the mark of pure birth. . . ." R. Judah in the name of Rav said, "If you see two people continually quarreling there is a blemish of unfitness in one of them, and they are [providentially] not allowed to cleave to each other."

(b. Qid. 71b)

Definitions were provided for genealogical purposes.

R. Papa in the name of Rav said, "Babylonia is healthy, Mesene is dead, Media is sick, and Elam is dying. What is the difference between the sick and the dying? The sick are destined for life, the dying for death."

(b. Qid. 71b)

Samuel held that Moxoene was genealogically as pure as Babylonia; Rav held that Halwan and Nehawand Jews were similarly "pure." In the same way the sickness of a region was determined by genealogies. Jews in whole provinces, however, ignored the rabbis' views, and as a result were declared heretic. Even in Babylonia itself existed substantial numbers of people whose ancestry, the rabbis alleged, concealed a marriage contrary to rabbinic law. The rabbis' knowledge of genealogy was regarded as thorough and sound. When Rav visited and examined a family, it was assumed he had studied their genealogy. Given the importance ascribed to inherited, as well as acquired, merits, one can easily understand how the "theological" importance of proper breeding played a significant part in peoples' choice of marriage partners. And yet even in Nehardea, a center of the rabbinic movement, were many families who had reason to fear rabbinic examination.

Few rabbis came from outlying regions, external to Babylonia itself. Elam, Mesene, Adiabene, Armenia, and elsewhere had no rabbinic schools and produced few disciples. The institutions and instruments for the propagation and application of rabbinic law were unavailable in those provinces. That is not to say Jews in the towns of Dura, Arbela, Tigranocerta, or Charax Spasinu were not "good Jews." They did keep the law as they understood it.

However, despite both the supernatural repute enjoyed by rabbis and their access to the coercive power available to the exilarch from the Iranian state, several factors stood in the way of the rabbis' and the exilarch's completely effective enforcement of the law and values of rabbinic Judaism. First, even the exilarch did not possess adequate means of physical coercion. Second, even if he had had the means, he was not the sole legal authority in Babylonia. He ruled only the affairs of his Babylonian Jewish subjects, while other groups and territories, including those with a substantial Jewish population, were not under his control. In addition, some Jews, having been excommunicated in a confrontation with rabbinic authority over Sabbath-breaking, simply abandoned Judaism and thus placed themselves beyond the pale of Jewish law. While this does not prove that the rabbis possessed *no* authority whatever, it does suggest that circumstances limited their effectiveness. Lacking armies or police and supported only by the *willingness* of Jews to obey the law because it had been revealed by God to Moses on Sinai and transmitted faithfully to their own generation, the rabbis had to resort to nonphysical means. In some measure they relied upon persuasion; in some, upon the inertial force of accepted authority; and in some, upon the willingness of the Persian government to accept their decrees. But mostly they were dependent upon the acquiescence of the people themselves. Because of the precariousness of any kind of government in an age in which the execution of law was slow and inefficient and might be impeded by factors out of the control of any Jewish authority, the mere proclamation of law meant little practically. This underlines the importance of courts and schools for effecting the social changes at which the rabbis aimed.

### iii. The Rabbi as Government Official

What did a rabbi actually do as a community administrator? The following account gives a helpful portrait of the workaday functions of R. Huna, head of the Sura academy, *ca.* A.D. 300:

"Every cloudy day they would carry him out in a golden palanquin, and he would survey the whole town. Every wall which looked unsafe he would order torn down. If the owner could rebuild it, he did so, but if not, he [R. Huna] would rebuild it of his own funds."

"On the eve of every Sabbath, he would send a messenger to the market, and all the vegetables that remained to the market-gardeners, he would buy and throw into the river."

"Whenever he discovered a medicine, he would fill a jug with it, and suspend it above the doorstep and announce, 'Whoever wants to, let him come and take.' Some say, he knew from tradition a medicine for [a certain disease caused by eating with unwashed hands], and he would suspend a jug of water and proclaim, 'Whoever needs it, let him come so that he may save his life from danger.' "

"When he ate bread, he would open his door wide and declare, 'Whoever is in need, let him come and eat.' "

(b. Ta. 20b-21a)

One is struck by the variety of public responsibilities carried out by the rabbi. He had to see to it that the mud-constructed buildings did not collapse after a rainstorm. He had to insure that a constant market was maintained by encouraging the truck-gardeners to provide a steady supply of fresh vegetables. He had to give out medical information, to preserve public health, and to make certain that poor people could benefit from the latest remedies. And he had to provide for the poor, so that no one would starve in his town.

These responsibilities reflected the different roles played by the rabbi. Only the first and second duties listed depended upon his political function. As judge he could order the destruction of dangerous property; as administrator he had to supervise the marketplace and use his funds to control supply and prices. But these roles had nothing to do with medical and eleemosynary activities. The former was contingent upon his reputation as a man of learning who had mastered the occult sciences, which then included medicine; the latter was based upon the fact that he possessed great wealth, accruing from his positions in politics, administration, and academic life. One must conclude, therefore, that as a community administrator the rabbi effected the various laws and Oral Traditions in several different ways. First was his coercive power, based upon the courts, but extending mostly to litigations over property and market transactions. Strictly speaking, he sought to carry out all the laws and to ensure the Jewish people's conformity to them, but it was only civil laws, torts, proper court procedures, and some economic dicta—not all of them derived from the rabbinic tradi-

107

tion—which were actually *enforced* by the rabbi. Second, the rabbi could *influence* ordinary Jews because of his reputation as a holy and learned man, his knowledge of medicine and magic, and his supposedly unusual "merit." It would be natural for ordinary people to accept his leadership, even when it was not based upon political or coercive agencies. Third, he could set a public example which others would be encouraged to emulate through promises of heavenly reward or punishment. Finally, in his academy, he could *decree* for his disciples precisely what he wanted.

### iv. ENFORCING THE LAW

While in some matters, only the curse, or the threat to cast an evil eye or withhold a blessing, or the promise of a reward effected rabbinical dicta, the rabbinical courts were not limited to merely inveighing against popular misconduct or appealing through personal influence for conformity to the ideals of the religious elite. The rabbis made no distinction between civil and religious law, and they tried to use whatever power their courts had to enforce both types. Each was revealed and equally holy; neither was considered inconsequential.

However, one needs to distinguish carefully between the beliefs which rendered the rabbis influential and the actual judicial power that effected their court decisions. Beliefs about the rabbis as miracle-workers must have provided them with considerable influence over the people, but in the numerous recorded cases of law enforcement in court there are none in which the rabbi was consulted because of his capacities to do things which we would regard as magical. Punishment was rarely meted out in any court case through theurgical means.

Supernatural influence was used mostly where legal power was unavailable and specifically in those matters of law which almost never produced cases and court action. People were cursed and died of the evil eye, or the rabbis' superior knowledge of genealogy was cited as an influence on popular behavior. If the rabbis declared that rain was withheld only because of neglect of the laws of tithing or because of neglect of Torah, they said so because they lacked better means of getting the people to give their tithes or to study the Torah. These two matters are not exactly comparable, for giving tithes was a matter of priestly property rights, while study of the

Torah was a more general and non-litigable matter. However, if in both kinds of law, threats of drought were invoked, it was because the rabbis lacked a more potent method.

Similarly, rabbis wielded enormous influence on account of their knowledge of genealogy. Rav Judah's son, Rami, said, "Since the book of genealogies has been hidden, the strength of the sages has been impaired and the light of their eyes dimmed." Obviously, if people believed the sages did not really know the genealogies, then their influence would have indeed diminished. Where the rabbis could exert very specific action, they did not merely threaten to talk of genealogies, but flogged.

The law was enforced in two ways; first, through intimidation or encouragement of the people, and second, through court actions or decrees. When Samuel told pot-sellers that they had better reduce the price for their pots or he would announce an interpretation of the law which would drastically reduce the demand for their product, he did not need to threaten that it would not rain, that they would not have male children, that their children would never study the Torah, or that he would reveal who their great-grandfather really was. All he had to do was say that he knew a law which was inimical to their interests, and that he could enforce it. That was sufficient, and no more "spiritual" measures were required in its place.

The actual means of law enforcement available to rabbinic courts were varied, but excluded capital punishment. In fact, during the period under study, only three capital cases were recorded. Rabbinical discussions on such issues as who provides the equipment for a capital punishment, how to select the appropriate means of execution among the several decreed by Jewish law, and the like were entirely theoretical.

There were four main punishments:

> When R. Huna would go to court he would say, "Bring me the instruments of my trade: the staff, and the strap, and the *shofar*, and the sandal."
>
> (b. Sanh. 7b)

The staff was for beating, the strap for the thirty-nine stripes of flagellation, the *shofar* (ram's horn) for excommunication, and the sandal for the ceremony of *ḥaliẓah* (a ceremony annulling the relationship between a childless woman and her deceased husband's brother). Of the four punishments, flogging was by far the most common, with excommunication second. R. Judah flogged a man who clipped the wings of a dam before letting go, and then caught it again. In this instance, the flogging was a "rabbinical" punishment. The rabbis distinguished between stripes, which were ordained by biblical law, and flogging, which the rabbis might inflict at their discretion.

Still another rabbinical punishment involved cutting off a hand:

R. Huna said, "[He who lifts up his hand against his neighbor] should have his hand cut off, as it is written, *Let the uplifted arm be broken* (Job 38:15) ."
R. Huna had the hand cut off.

(b. Sanh. 58b)

R. Huna obviously took a biblical curse literally. In another case he inflicted a similar penalty on one who masturbated. Other rabbis used different punishments. Rav said that one who willfully caused an erection should be excommunicated, while R. Ammi maintained that he would not be allowed to enter the division of the Holy One. Rav Judah ordered a man who committed incest with his mother-in-law to be flogged, and R. Sheshet did so to a man who merely passed by the door of his father-in-law's house.

The ban was used under various circumstances. If a disciple were irritated by an outsider, or if he irritated his master, the culprit was put under the ban for one day, although no formal proceeding was undertaken. Whole communities were banned at times. For example, R. Hamnuna saw people at work when he thought that they should be accompanying a corpse for burial, and he banned them until he later learned that they were not so obligated. The ban, however, was not effective over large groups, for it depended upon the cooperation of all law-abiding people.

R. Ḥisda said, "A butcher who is a priest and does not give the priestly dues [to another priest] is to be excommunicated from the God of Israel."
Rabbah b. R. Shila said, "The butchers of Huẓal have been under R. Ḥisda's ban for the past twenty-two years."

(b. Ḥul. 132b)

Whether R. Ḥisda actually issued such a decree or not is not clear from the saying of Rabbah b. R. Shila, for it may be that the actions of the butchers quite automatically brought the excommunication without a formal decree. But the important fact is that the butchers as a group seemed able to thrive for twenty-two years despite it. A recalcitrant individual undoubtedly would have had much greater difficulty.

The rabbis were aware that the effectiveness of rabbinic law enforcement relied upon the cooperation of the whole community, and that they were limited by that fact. An individual could usually be brought into line rather easily either by the force of public opinion or by judicial action. However, if the community could not, or would not, obey the rabbinic decree, then the rabbi was best advised not to issue it in the first place, and so R. Adda b. Ahva said: "One may not issue a decree unless the majority of the community can abide by it" (b. A.Z. 36a-b). As in the case of the butchers of Huzal, law enforcement was impossible in the face of massive public disobedience.

In enforcing the law, the rabbis played a dualistic role. First, they acted as agents of the exilarch, judging cases brought before the Jewish autonomous government. On the other hand, they saw themselves as authorized not by the exilarch but by their own mastery of Torah to govern the affairs of the Jewish people. As exilarchic agents, they were authorized to do certain things, and these included the punishments prepared by R. Huna for his court sessions. However, the rabbis also wanted to enforce laws of no relevance to the exilarchate's political and administrative responsibilities. In such cases they used their moral, rather than their legal, powers of persuasion; without the exilarch's support, they had no better means available. When they acted wholly on their own, they had to rely upon threats and promises of worldly and supernatural recompense rather than upon the staff, the strap, the *shofar,* and the sandal. Four different circumstances of rabbinical law enforcement are discernible. The first was illustrated above. When everyone did the right thing—or the wrong thing—the rabbis had no role whatever, and some thought it unnecessary or futile even to announce the law.

The second was the most common: most people obeyed the law, but a few did not. This condition would permit application of the ban of excommunication, or beating for rebellion against rabbinical authority or scriptural law, or the normal procedures of law, such as the *halizah* ceremony. Included also were the everyday litigations of a vigorous community where the rabbinical courts were resorted

111

to by all manner of people for quite normal and everyday adjudications.

The third circumstance involved matters such as capital or other major crimes which the rabbis were not permitted by the imperial government to administer. These probably were referred to the Iranian government for action.

The fourth was composed of non-litigable concerns of public faith and morals, ethical concerns in which rabbinical dicta could not be enforced but could only be advocated as a matter of right action or right belief. Here the rabbis could exert their considerable spiritual and moral prestige, and warn of dire consequences which the very processes of nature would bring down upon the head of the sinner. They could even warn that improper behavior was standing in the way of the coming of the Messiah.

Two exceptions to this structuring of public behavior require specification. First was the Jew who either separated himself completely from Judaism and the community or who threw off the internal self-discipline characteristic of the community as a whole. An example was the informer, who dealt with the Persian authorities not through the usual channels of the autonomous government, but directly and secretively. R. Huna and Rav Judah debated on whether it was permitted to destroy his property directly, and whether an offense against that property would be worse than one against his body. The contemporary Palestinian opinion was that an informer, an apostate, and a *min* (heretic) could be thrown into a well and not brought up, although there are no records of cases in which such a punishment actually happened.

The rabbis had to struggle not only with heretics, but also with lawless people in general. The Babylonian Jews were reputed in Palestine to be particularly violent and ungovernable, as the following story indicates:

When 'Ulla traveled to the land of Israel, he was accompanied by two men of Khuzistan. One arose and slew his fellow.
He said to 'Ulla, "Did I do well?"
He replied, "Yes, and cut his throat clean across."
When he arrived before R. Yoḥanan, he said to him, "Perhaps, God forbid, I have strengthened the hands of transgressors?"
He replied, "You saved your life."
He was amazed however: "Is it not written, *And the Lord shall give them there an angry heart* (Deut. 28:65) which refers to Babylonia?"

[How then could they have done so in Palestine?] 'Ulla answered, "At that time we had not yet crossed the Jordan."

(b. Ned. 22)

The above case, involving mere violence and not heresy or disloyalty, suggests how difficult would be the task of anyone who sought to enforce order in Jewry.

The second major obstacle to law enforcement concerned treatment of the wealthy. Rabbis had to set aside normal legal procedures to counteract the power of rich and influential Jews, who could ignore rabbinical authority and act pretty much as they chose. One such rich man, R. Ḥana b. Ḥanilai, was warmly praised by the rabbis 'Ulla and R. Ḥisda:

> When once 'Ulla and R. Ḥisda were walking along the road, they came to the door of the house of R. Ḥana b. Ḥanilai. R. Ḥisda broke down and sighed.
>
> Said 'Ulla to him, "Why are you sighing, seeing that Rav has said that a sigh breaks half a man's body . . . ?"
>
> He replied, "How shall I refrain from sighing on seeing the house in which there used to be sixty cooks by day and sixty cooks by night, who cooked for everyone who was in need. Nor did he [R. Ḥana] ever take his hand away from his purse, thinking that perhaps a respectable poor man might come, and while he was getting his purse he would be put to shame. Moreover it had four doors, opening on different sides, and whoever went in hungry went out full. They used also to throw wheat and barley outside in years of scarcity, so that anyone who was ashamed to take by day used to come and take by night. Now it has fallen in ruins, and shall I not sigh?"
>
> He replied to him, "Thus said R. Yoḥanan, 'Since the day when the Temple was destroyed, a decree has been issued against the houses of the righteous that they shall become desolate.' "

(b. Ber. 58b)

The righteous rich became desolate. Others, not so meticulous in their moral and religious duties, doubtless made considerable trouble for rabbis, who were comforted by the thought that, to begin with, no really righteous man had ever remained rich since A.D. 70. It may be inferred from a story such as this one about the very rare, pious rich man, how much difficulty the rabbis had even in the towns in which the academies and courts were actually located. In the end the most severe obstacle to rabbinic rule must have been the anarchy which at times rendered any government—Jewish or Iranian—irrelevant to the day-to-day affairs of its people.

Public acquiescence to both rabbinic and exilarchic rule was decisive. The Jews believed that Moses had revealed God's will on Sinai, and that they were required to carry out his will. In general most of the Jews kept the law because they believed that it was their obligation to Heaven to do so and not because of the threats or promises of the exilarch or his rabbinical judges. It was the common faith in the Bible as revealed by God that brought the masses under the influence—as well as under the specific administrative authority —of the political and legal institutions. The Jews could easily apostatize to the dominant faith, the Sasanians' Zoroastrianism, or to a competing biblical faith in Babylonia, either Mandaeanism or Christianity, or even to Manichaeism. Some did convert to the Sasanian faith, and a number of Jews did become Christians in these times, although there is no evidence of apostasy to other cults or religions. Therefore, remaining within the Jewish community represented an act of faith in the basic principles of Judaism, and that act entailed submission which was the basis for the effectuation of the entire system of enforcement of the rabbinic laws.

v.  The People and the Torah

Mosaic revelation shaped the religious life of the masses. The rabbis did not need to urge the people to keep fundamental, biblically ordained laws. The people did keep the laws because they believed it was what God wanted them to do. Popular practice required rabbinical supervision of the ways the commandments were to be carried out. On matters where biblical laws and rabbinical interpretations were perfectly clear, well-known, and widely accepted, the rabbis were able to guide the affairs of the people who brought them their queries. This was done without need of coercion of any kind. On the other hand, where rabbinical injunctions were more severe, or not widely known, the rabbis had to rely upon a measure of coercion, as best they could. For the most part, however, the rabbis were *consulted* by the people, because they were believed to know precisely the way the law should be obeyed. Therefore, in commonplace areas of law, they did not have to resort to floggings, excommunication, and the like.

This is not to suggest that the masses were quite so meticulously observant of the laws as the rabbis would have liked, or that even in some elementary matters the law was easily enforced. R. Aḥai b. R. Josiah (*ca.* A.D. 150) had to excommunicate a whole village because of Sabbath violation. Tension between a class of religious virtuosi and the masses of their followers was certainly not an uncommon phenomenon in the history of religions. However, because of their biblical knowledge the Jewish masses provided an example of a community which, on the whole, proved amenable to the guidance of their leaders—even when those leaders modified long-established customs, as long as such actions could be based on exegeses of Scriptures. It was, in the end, the schoolhouse which guided and defined obedience to the law.

The three kinds of laws most rigorously obeyed by the people were those of *Kashrut* (the various dietary rules and taboos), menstrual separation, and the Sabbath. Obviously, the rabbis could not supervise every kitchen in Babylonia to be sure the dietary laws were obeyed. Generally they either had to wait to be consulted about the law or tried to enforce it out-of-hand in the butcher shops if they could. When consulted, they could, of course, issue decrees which the people, if they wanted to do the right thing, might carry out.

The laws governing the cessation of intercourse during a woman's menstrual period were equally difficult to enforce except by voluntary action; if the rabbis could not inspect every farm and every kitchen, they most certainly could not supervise every bedroom. However, the people did consult rabbinical authority with frequency, and thus conscientiously sought to obey the menstrual taboos.

Although rabbis were frequently consulted in all three types of laws, it was mainly in matters pertaining to Sabbath observance that they had to resort to floggings for violations. Unlike the preceding laws, Sabbath observance was a public event; violations, therefore, were also public. The rabbis did not have to wait to be consulted. They aggressively punished Sabbath breaking, and because of well-known biblical precedents, the people doubtless expected them to. Although the rabbis used physical coercion to ensure proper Sabbath observance in their own communities, it is not known how the Sabbath law was observed in areas not under rabbinical supervision. Numerous inquiries to rabbis came from rabbinical stu-

115

dents, however, whose Sabbath observance would have carried the rabbis' influence far beyond the limits of their supervision.

By contrast, the synagogue liturgies were not invariably conducted according to rabbinical opinion. The rabbi had no special function in synagogue affairs. He did not preside over the service, nor was his presence necessary for its conduct. Any Jew was able to lead the prayers and read from the Torah.

The rabbinical distinction between laws revealed by Moses at Sinai and laws decreed by the rabbis was important for Babylonia, for the people accepted the former, but had to be taught the latter. In matters not susceptible to court intervention, the latter must have had little impact upon common people whenever the old traditions of Babylonia were in contradiction or merely silent. Thus R. Joseph remarked that the paragraph in the Grace after Meals concerning God's goodness (ending ". . . who is good and does good") must not be scriptural in origin, "for working people omit it from the Grace." The converse is that if it were of scriptural origin, working people presumably would include it. Actually not much can be proved from a single saying, for whether ordinary folk said the Grace after Meals in a manner similar to the rabbinical formulation (or indeed whether they recited grace at all) is hardly settled. What is important is R. Joseph's supposition that working people ordinarily would know and carry out biblical ordinances but not rabbinical ones.

If his supposition was sound, then the reason must have been the perseverance of patterns of religious life from olden times, long before the arrival in Babylonia of the first Pharisaic masters and the foundation of rabbinical schools in the second century A.D. Before the coming of rabbinical Judaism, Babylonian Jewry must have developed a rich cultural and religious life based upon reverence for the Scriptures, the Jerusalem Temple, and Yahweh, and upon *ad hoc* interpretations of Scriptures and legal decisions by local elders. The rabbis used their claim to possess Mosaic traditions unavailable elsewhere as their justification for reforming Jewish community life.

It was through the courts that the sages exercised their most direct and effective power over ordinary Jews. Yet the courts' authority was severely circumscribed. Apart from enforcing civil laws concerning property and making decisions on personal status—marriage, divorce —which depended upon exchanges of property, the courts could only sporadically coerce obedience to Torah. Even though Torah comprehended a wide range of teachings about the proper conduct of everyday life, the sages through the courts affected only a small part of daily affairs.

The reasons for the rabbis' limited use of their court powers for enforcement of the "whole Torah"—both the written and the oral —are clear. The Iranian government, first of all, did not leave in the hand of the autonomous minority communities an unlimited range of power. Cases involving large sums of money, major crimes, capital punishment, and the like were reserved for the Iranian courts. Furthermore, the rabbinical courts' powers were circumscribed by the probability that other courts also exercised jurisdiction over Jews.

Competing authorities were likely to have been of three sorts. First, towns mainly inhabited by Jews but not the center of rabbinical schools were governed by non-rabbinical authorities, composed of officials such as the ignorant judges about whom the rabbis complained. Although such judges probably were also subject to the authority of the exilarch, they obviously were not educated in rabbinical schools or governed by the discipline of the rabbinical estate.

Second, the rabbis did not have the power to decide cases involving substantial sums of money, capital punishment, or other weighty matters. Hence either the exilarch or the Iranian government, acting through local satraps, took jurisdiction over many types of important legal and administrative matters affecting ordinary Jews. The exilarch presided over the only murder trial mentioned in Babylonian rabbinical records. The rabbis concentrated attention on the *disposition* of stolen goods. They did not mention what happened to the thief. Presumably a higher authority punished him.

The third and most important type of authority which competed with the rabbis was the Iranian courts. Cases involving Jews and gentiles rarely, if ever, seem to have come before rabbinical courts. Since large numbers of Jews lived in Seleucia-Ctesiphon (Maḥoza) and other places where they were likely to come into contact with gentiles, to enter into business partnerships, and otherwise to produce litigation, the state had to make provision for disputes among its mixed populations.

Obviously, even though rabbis did make some sorts of decisions, one ought not to exaggerate the extent of their control over the lives of ordinary Jews. The cases before the rabbinical courts were

117

the exceptional ones in which people deprived others of their property or rights, failed to keep their word, or otherwise lapsed from accepted norms. Under usual circumstances the courts played no role whatever, though, conversely, the law itself played a great role indeed. Furthermore, if "heretics are common who vex the rabbis," and if the men of Nersh "would not hear the word of the Lord," then it may be supposed the sages' power also was limited by the difficulties of coercing independent-minded Jews to conform at all. People usually kept civil law; however, they probably did pretty much as they pleased unless they actually came into direct conflict either with another person's rights or property, or with a rabbinical authority who was engaged in the exercise of his duties. It would have required far more efficient government than existed in late antiquity, combined with a vast and inquisitive police force, to impose the whole Torah upon all of Babylonian Jewry. What could readily be imposed was a rather small segment of the law— civil litigations and determinations of personal status. The law could come to bear mostly when ordinary Jews brought one another to court in a litigation. So in the end, even judgments of civil law and determinations of personal status by rabbis generally depended upon the compliance of the people.

Central to the concern of and certainly subject to the authority of sages were many kinds and patterns of human relationships. While rabbis had little influence over "religion," they had a great deal of influence over "ethics." But no one at that time would have made such a distinction. Behavior in the marketplace as much as in the synagogue constituted a matter of Torah. Indeed the rabbis rightly saw themselves as heirs of the teachings of the prophets, their best interpreters and true continuators. For this reason they devoted themselves to commonplace justice, doing what they could, to be sure, about the sancta and taboos as well. Effecting a reconciliation between husband and wife; preserving the sanctity of marital ties; properly carrying out betrothals, marriages, and, where appropriate, divorces; protecting the rights of women by providing for their maintenance—these represented human relationships potentially subject to rabbinical control, and therefore, to rabbinical judgments or values. Likewise, "the Holy One" who knew the difference "between the first born and others in Egypt" would also know the difference between honest and dishonest traders. The rabbis would remind marketmen of that fact, forcibly so when they

118

were able to make effective rulings over what was done in bailments and contracts, exchanges of commerce, trade, movables, transactions over land, settlement of estates, and similar matters. Rabbinical ideas about human rights might not invariably coincide with those of today. But in general when it came to property disputes, theirs was a fair standard of justice, and, more important, it was also a quick and effective one.

## vi. THE COURTS

Litigations coming before the Jewish courts were not particularly important; on the whole they corresponded to those likely to come before a small-claims court in modern society. Thefts involved a book or a few rams. Betrothal cases concerned the exchange of property, such as a few zuz, a willow branch, some onions, or a piece of silk. Settlements of marriage contracts required division of a robe of fine wool, a silver cup. A few cases of alleged adultery were recorded, all of sufficient innocence for the court to rule that no adultery had taken place. Ceremonies of halizah and the preparation and delivery of proper divorce documents hardly amounted to weighty matters of state. Divorce litigations in any event were provoked by peculiar and exceptional circumstances; normally a man could divorce his wife without court intervention, merely with the help of a scribe who wrote out the writ of divorce in accordance with the law.

The settlement of estates entailed somewhat larger sums of money. A woman's marriage contract stipulated that if she were divorced, she would be given an alimony of four hundred zuz, a round number which probably represented approximately enough capital for two years' maintenance. Provisions by the court for widows (food, wine, clothing) were humble and more typical matters. Even most estate cases pertained to rather small claims, such as a few trees, a slave, or a choice plot of ground. Settlement of debts, collections of mortgages and bonds, and the like did require rulings on somewhat more substantial sums, but the real issues were still relatively inconsequential—a hundred zuz, or whether a pledged spoon or knife had to be returned.

Some commercial litigations were brought before the courts. Broken contracts were entered into by a few ferrymen and sharecroppers, or devolved upon a hired ass, the purchase of some wine or poppy seed, a flooded field. Some commercial disputes demanded that the courts decide about a few *zuz* worth of silk beads, some sour wine, the sale of a wine press or of a field. Others concerned damages done to a jar or utensil, a dead goat, a silver cup, a purse of money stolen in part through negligence, a broken ax and a broken wine barrel. Property cases similarly involved alleged fraud in a relatively small plot, the supposed existence of an option to purchase a field, the use of some canal water, and very frequently, squatter's rights over a house or a field which the owner had not seen for some time and the eviction of tenant farmers.

Cases such as these clearly reveal the real substance of issues left in the rabbis' hands. With a few exceptions, strikingly petty sums of money or barely consequential amounts of property were all that the courts actually adjudicated. Since these were mainly affairs of the lower classes of society, it was those classes that were primarily subject to rulings by the rabbinical courts. Large commercial transactions for many thousands of *zuz* worth of silk or pearls, wine or beer; enormous property transactions involving a whole village or town; claims of a considerable number of workers against a single employer, or vice versa; the affairs of large estates, rich landowners, big businessmen, important officials—none of these appear with any frequency, if at all, in the reports available today. The reason was only partly that not many Jews seem to have been located in the higher strata of society. Another factor to be considered is that the rabbinical courts' jurisdiction undoubtedly was limited. The absence of significant criminal actions (apart from the single murder case before the exilarch) indicates that some authority other than the rabbinical courts was responsible for criminal prosecutions. It is likely that the exilarch held the chief responsibility—unless the Sasanian courts retained it for themselves—for anything really important.

The rabbis surely could not have agreed, however, that the humble and petty issues before them were of no consequence. It was their view—a very old one in Judaism—that the least and humblest affairs, as much as the largest and most weighty ones, testified to heaven about the moral state of society. If the prophet Amos had condemned Israel of old because a poor man was cheated of his shoes, then one can hardly be surprised that a later rabbi insisted upon the return of a cooking utensil given in pledge. What was important to the rabbis was that justice should prevail. They knew that if justice did not characterize the street, the trading market, the small farms and shops, then great affairs of commerce and the state would not likely be morally superior. It has already been stressed that the ethics of daily life—the life consisting of exchanges of onions and the use of water in a small canal—determined the destiny of Israel, according to rabbinic theology. Therefore, the petty cases settled by courts controlled by the rabbis mattered very much to them.

A curious contrast can be observed between observance of the laws concerning ritual matters and cases dealing with personal status and property transactions. A study of the former clearly shows that through their political position rabbis could do little, if anything, to enforce, or even to guide, the observance of many laws related to the Sabbath and festivals; holy objects; taboos about sex, food, and clothing; and the like. Exceptions to this rule are explicable in terms of the rabbis' public position. As they supervised the market-places, they were able to determine what kind of meat and wine was suitable for sale and what was not. Thus they could instruct the butcher and supervise the abattoirs. In their role as communal officials, they could see to it that the Sabbath-limits were properly established. They did not have to wait to be consulted, but simply went and carried out the law as they saw fit.

However, having no special place in the synagogue, the rabbis as community officials had more influence over the disposition of synagogue property than over the rites and prayers normally carried on there. They could preach and so acquired some further influence over the ordinary people through public instruction in the synagogue. But that influence cannot be confused with power exerted by public officials and judges. The extensive legal discussions about Grace after Meals, prayers to be said on various special occasions, Sabbath and festival rites and taboos, the preparation of the home for Passover, the conduct of the Passover *Seder,* building the *Sukkah* (tabernacle), observance of the New Year and the Day of Atonement, special fast days, reading the Scroll of Esther on the holiday of Purim, conduct on the intermediate days of festivals, not to mention the whole range of laws dealing with other aspects of ritual life —few if any of these discussions produce such significant exemplifications of popular obedience as to persuade one that ordinary people were much affected by them.

It is curious that, while the Babylonian rabbinical courts could easily determine proper judicial procedures, decide on how documents were to be drawn up, and determine the rules of evidence and oath-taking, by contrast the Talmudic discussions on the laws of the Sanhedrin and the structure of Jewish judiciary do not indicate that those courts were set up according to rabbinic tradition. The exilarch evidently organized the courts and administration without reference to pertinent rabbinical traditions. Once established, however, those courts were run as the rabbis wanted.

In matters of personal status, the view of the rabbis was enforced in courts, and therefore prevailed widely. For example, public recognition of the legality of a marriage and the legitimacy of its offspring depended upon court action, not merely upon private acquiescence; since the rabbis were in charge of the courts, their views gained ascendancy. Earlier it was observed that in territories where people were indifferent to rabbinical laws, there was little rabbis could do but prohibit Jewish marriages with the inhabitants and, where appropriate, declare the offspring illegitimate. In Babylonia, however, the rabbis' power and authority were much more substantial, and their courts possessed great prestige. There are reports of many cases where either the rabbis were consulted or their laws put into effect in matters of personal status, marriage, and divorce, and in the preparation of documents relevant to such affairs. The law on these subjects reflects practical, and not only theoretical, situations.

The rabbis issued public instructions (sometimes contradictory) in matters of marriage, but whether they were invariably obeyed is not known. Although Rav taught that a barren marriage must be annulled after two and one-half years, there is no record of a single case in which such a law was applied. The normal means of law enforcement in cases of personal status was flogging:

Rav ordered the chastisement of any person who betrothed by cohabitation [rather than by a document or money-exchange], who betrothed in the open street, or who betrothed without previous negotiation; who annulled a letter of divorce, or who made a declaration against [the validity of] a letter of divorce; who was insolent towards the representative of the Rabbis, or who allowed a Rabbinical ban upon him to remain for thirty days and did not come to the [court] to request the removal of that ban; and of a son-in-law who lives in his father-in-law's house.

. . . The Nehardeans stated: "Rav ordered the chastisement of none of these except him who betrothed by cohabitation without preliminary negotiation [because this was sheer licentiousness]."

(b. Yev. 52a)

It seems most reasonable to accept the view of the Nehardeans. The other cases given in the first paragraph would have involved the flogging of people who, without any evil intent, had probably acted in a way they thought right (except for those who did not heed the decree of a rabbinical court, and these may have been so numerous that flogging would have been required everywhere, bringing the law and the rabbis into disrepute).

The rabbinical courts thus administered laws pertaining to the marketplace, including the abattoir, and supervised the collection and division of funds for the poor. They had no difficulty in overseeing commercial life, ascertaining that butchers slaughtered and sold meat in conformity with Jewish ritual requirements, and exercising other functions relevant to public welfare. The courts took full responsibility for the establishment of the Sabbath limits, entirely within their control as communal administrative agencies. Certain other kinds of law were probably carried out according to rabbinical rules because rabbis were presumed to know what Scriptures required. These laws pertained to a few agricultural offerings and gifts to priests, taboos against sexual relations with a menstruating woman, and the like. The rabbis' reputation as men of great learning, rather than their position in the courts, probably accounts for their success in guiding popular observance of those particular laws.

That same reputation, however, seems to have had little or no effect upon other religious rites. Rabbinical rules about mourning; the observance of holy days, festivals, and the Sabbath (except for the laws of 'eruvin [Sabbath boundaries]) ; the preparation and use of amulets, charms, and holy objects—these produced little or no impact upon popular behavior. People buried their dead, kept the Jewish festivals, resorted to amulets to guard their houses from demons, prepared and read sacred Scrolls, and the like, but the role rabbis played in these matters, if any, is simply not revealed by the evidence at hand today. If no stories existed about what *anyone*— rabbi or common people—actually did and there were no case reports or records of inquiries to the rabbis from ordinary Jews, then no hypothesis whatever could be offered. There is, however, a considerable body of evidence on the enforcement of some laws, but none at all about others. Surely if cases on those others had arisen, stories about them would have been preserved; since none are, it may be supposed the reason was that Jews outside of the schools neither kept, nor even cared about, these particular rabbinical laws.

The rabbinical courts, therefore, served mainly to administer public affairs and had slight direct impact upon the homes and synagogues of common people. The original agreement between the exilarch, through Samuel, and the Sasanians in the time of Shapur I had specified that the Jewish courts would not transgress Persian law. The cases cited in connection with Samuel's pronouncement that Sasanian government law was to be obeyed had involved the payment of taxes, the adjudication of property rights which included the status of heathen property, and the means by which property was acquired. In ritual matters, the Jewish courts were probably left free to decide as they liked—if they could. It is hard to see how the Persian government would have cared whether or not rabbis told ordinary Jews what to do on the Sabbath. So if the rabbis' power over ritual life seems to have been narrowly restricted to public, administrative roles, the exilarch, and not the Persians, would have set that restriction. For the exilarch, the rabbis served as useful court officials. Their knowledge of law purported to have been given by Moses was considerable. Although the rabbis formed a disciplined, dependable party, the exilarch was probably opposed to their making unrestricted use of the courts to control people's behavior. It was one thing to care for the poor, to collect taxes, and to preserve an orderly and ritually acceptable market. It was quite another to intervene in the private lives of people.

An observation of the contrast in Sabbath laws is suggestive. If ordinary Jews liked, they could consult the rabbis about keeping the Sabbath, and occasionally some people did so. But if they were not consulted, the rabbis apparently had little power to punish people who, from their viewpoint, had sinned; Sabbath limits meant nothing to people who did not want to be guided by them. On the other hand, the rabbis' public position as community administrators left them free to set up legal Sabbath boundaries. Had ordinary people simply ignored the Sabbath and gone about their daily business, the rabbis, as administrators, would surely have punished them—and the people would have expected them to do so. It is likely, therefore, that very few people actually did violate the laws. There was one area where rabbinical power was necessary but lacking: the middle ground between the rare public violation of the biblical rules against work and the unopposed public administration of rabbinical rules about the Sabbath limit. This area included such matters as what people wore or carried on the Sabbath or how they prepared food at home. These were the kinds of things that the exilarch felt were essentially private and, therefore, should be beyond rabbinical regulation.

This is not to suggest that an individual's religious observance would greatly have varied from that of the community in which he lived. Such a supposition would be an anachronism. What was from the court's perspective "private"—that is, beyond court authority—was, from both the exilarch's and the people's viewpoint, most probably the accustomed way of doing things. The pre-rabbinic patterns of Babylonian Judaism must have been deeply rooted. These were doubtless shaped by biblical laws and local customs, *ad hoc* decisions, and ancient, accepted exegeses of Scriptures. For many centuries Babylonian Jews had kept the Sabbath and festivals, offered synagogue prayers and read the Torah, buried the dead, and observed other rites, laws, and taboos. The exilarch was hardly prepared to allow the disruption of popular and accepted practices or to provoke a revolution among the masses. So if, as seems clear, the rabbis' control over many rites was slight (except in such ways as the people invited their rulings), the reason was that the exilarch did not find it in the public interest to allow rabbinical intervention.

## vii. FROM SCHOOLHOUSE TO SOVEREIGNTY

For the rabbis, the limited control they enjoyed at that time could not have been satisfactory. They did not regard the laws about civil damages and torts as more holy than those about prayers or the Sabbath. It was simply that circumstances permitted them to enforce the former in court, but only to teach about the latter in school. The reason they acquiesced in an only partially acceptable situation was that they hoped in time to improve it. They could not have aspired to less than complete, public, communal conformity to the whole Torah, both the written part, which all the people knew, and the oral traditions only the rabbis then possessed. They chose to cooperate with the exilarchate to enforce as much of the law as they could—and dared. But in time, they intended to reconstruct Jewish community life so that the whole Torah would pertain, so far as relevant. And when they did succeed, they fully expected that all of it *would* be relevant, for on that day the Messiah would come, the Temple would be rebuilt, and the Jewish people would be restored to their own land and to their own government. Meanwhile, they wanted to construct as full a replica of that ideal situation as was possible before redemption, so as to hasten and effect that redemption. The rabbinic school, like the monastery of the nearby Christian community, would provide the opportunity. There the Torah was studied and carried out in all possible detail by the masters and disciples. In the school, man in the image of God, and society in the paradigm of the heavenly academy, were to be embodied. And from the school, students and masters would go forth to exemplify the will of God, eventually to reshape the life of the streets, homes, farms, and marketplace to conform to it.

It is remarkable that the rabbis were able to see themselves as lawyers and politicians at all. They exercised no sovereignty; the state was alien. Outside pressure from the Iranian government laid stress upon keeping a peaceful and orderly community, but certainly not upon keeping to the laws of Moses exactly as the rabbis in particular expounded them. Thus the cohesion of the Jewish community produced by external pressure did not in any way depend upon, or result in faith in, the supremacy of *rabbinic* law. The state lent a measure of sovereignty to an exilarch from whom the rabbis were increasingly alienated. To the rabbis, the state gave no sovereignty whatever, nor in effect did the exilarch. The schools were their nation, and rule over them constituted their real sovereignty. If rabbinical laws were academic laws, for their part rabbis made no distinction between theoretical and practical law, nor did they recognize as final or acceptable a disjuncture between sacred law and the reality of actual practice. When rabbinic Judaism first determined to conquer a nation through the steady extension of its concept of the school to all of national life cannot be said. But it was when the previous Jewish state lost all semblance of sovereignty with the fall of Jerusalem in A.D. 70 that Yoḥanan b. Zakkai had actually made the schoolhouse into the sole legitimate instrumentality of Jewish sovereignty. From that time onward, sovereignty as others knew it began to pass out of the hands of other Jewish powers and into the houses of study, so far as the rabbis were concerned. In time, the rabbis proved in practice to be quite correct.

## viii. Conclusion

The fact that the rabbinical estate could accomplish not so little but so much is astonishing. When the first rabbis came to Babylonia shortly after the Bar Kokhba War, they had no basis for affecting, even interfering in, local affairs. They constituted an outgrowth of a Palestinian party, the Pharisees, then several centuries old. It is doubtful that they earlier had any significant following in Babylonia. Like the Essenes and other Jewish sects, they claimed Moses had founded their group and revealed its peculiar laws and doctrines. But unlike others, they both actively and successfully sought the power to make their claims effective in the everyday life of ordinary Jews. In so doing, they worked to change all Jews into rabbis and to reshape the community according to the model of their own sect. At the outset in Babylonia they enjoyed the support of the exilarch, a relatively new authority set in charge of Babylonian Jewry about a half-century earlier. The first refugee-rabbis in Babylonia were not an unknown quantity, but perhaps were encouraged to settle permanently in the ancient community. They possessed substantial legal traditions and were men of considerable education. Their internal discipline made them suitable for use in the effective administration of a group of far-flung communities. Because of their claim to be holy men, to possess the whole Torah, and to be the teachers of God's will for Israel, and because of the ability of some rabbis to authenticate these claims through "miracles," they could exercise influence based upon spiritual, not merely physical, coercion. Understanding this, the exilarch probably allied himself with the rabbinate in his attempts to overcome the power of local antecedent, traditional authorities of the old Babylonian Jewish communities.

It was in the end an uneven contest. To be sure, the local powers were known and habitually obeyed, but the force of inertial obedience was overcome in a short time by the well-organized and well-disciplined sages, who were backed by the exilarch and, through him, by the Parthian and the Sasanian regimes. The unification of political power within Jewry corresponded to the effort of both Iranian dynasties to organize a single central effective government subject to the control of Ctesiphon. Against the combined force of the imperial government, the authority of the exilarch, and the lawyer-magicians who were court judges and administrators backed by both, the preexisting local authorities could hardly prevail.

127

The rabbis quickly established their characteristic institution, the school, which over generations transformed ordinary Jews not merely into good lawyers and administrators, but rather into rabbis imbued with the convictions, adhering to the singular customs, and educated in the traditions of the rabbinical estate. The schools certainly proved substantial local influences (which were quite apart from the influences of the court system) where they were located and wherever their graduates lived. Thus, they constituted the second major force—with the courts being the first—for the expansion of rabbinical power. In many ways they were the more important of the two.

Throughout the third and fourth centuries, the schools increased in strength. Local academies related to the great schools known through the Babylonian Talmud must have multiplied. However, outside of a few larger centers where the major academies were located, the rabbinical disciples could not have constituted a majority in any one place. In all, the leading authorities and local disciples could by no means have formed a majority of Babylonian Jewry even by the end of Sasanian times. But the fact that the handful of masters existing *ca.* A.D. 140 had become by A.D. 640 so powerful a force as to affect all Babylonian Judaism and to dominate a substantial and important part of its everyday affairs remains extraordinary.

If, in addition to the Babylonian Talmud, there existed today a considerable body of information about the life of Babylonian Jewry —information that derived, for instance, from business documents, exilarchic archives, local chronicles, biographies, martyrologies, poetry, synagogue ruins, liturgies, records, papyri and ostraca, coins, other artifacts, Iranian government papers, and the like—then the present view of the history of Babylonian Judaism would certainly be far broader and deeper. But it could not be much different. The focus of interest would still have to be the relationships between a small group of rabbis and a large mass of people, the creative symbiosis of the organized, active, patient, disciplined few, and the inchoate, stubborn, passive, preoccupied many. This is not a new theme in the history of religions or of men's societies, but it seems to be played out in an exceptional, perhaps in a unique, way in the history of Babylonian Judaism.

# Chapter Five

———◆———

# Babylonian Judaism in Its Historical Setting

### i. Rabbi, Magus, Monk

Like other "holy men," the rabbi played political, religious, and cultural roles. Just as the Zoroastrian Magus was involved in the administration of the local community, in the maintenance of cultic life, and in the study and teaching of Mazdean beliefs and scriptures, so too was the rabbi. The difference, however, was that while the Magus never aspired to overthrow or subvert the Sasanian dynasty, but only to serve as a significant and influential part of its administration and to constitute its religious arm, the rabbis wanted to independently exercise quite direct and substantial power over the Jewish community. Such a difference probably was not readily discernible during this period, for it was apparently only Geniva who acted according to these aspirations. Nevertheless, the lines were drawn, and the direction of rabbinical policy was quite clear. On the one side were rabbis such as Naḥman who would correspond to the priest-politician Kartir, "the soul-savior of [Emperor] Bahram." Such rabbis were part of the Jewish established government, shared its values and aspirations, and served its purposes. They would represent the closest parallel to the leading Magi. On the other were Geniva and those who shared his disdain for, and suspicion of, the Davidic exilarch. To these there was no clear counterpart among the Magi.

A more significant comparison could be drawn to the Christian "religious," the monastic figures who dominated the Christian faith east of the Euphrates and shaped its character. Unlike the Christian monks, it was the aspiration of the rabbi *not* to form a separate society. He kept to himself very little. He did not live in a tight little eschatological community, confidently awaiting the day on which the sinners would know that he was right and they were wrong. For all his sense of forming part of an elite, he did not look upon the rest of the Jewish community as outsiders, less "elect" than himself. At many important points he shared the fundamental convictions of the broader community; what he most wanted was to teach the people how to live up to these convictions as *he* understood them. So if he was not a sectarian, the reason was that he aspired to a wider influence than other religious leaders. He wanted all the Jews to become rabbis. He asked *nothing* of himself that he regarded as inapplicable to others, and nothing of others that did not pertain to himself.

Herein lies a paradox of the rabbinical "estate." On the one hand, it was separate and, by its own standard, superior. On the other, it hoped to obliterate the distinctions between the rabbinate and other Jews, and believed that every Jew was equally able to achieve "superiority." So its aspiration to political power, so partisan and subversive of existing authority, represented a perfectly natural extension of its self-understanding. It was through politics that the rest of Jewry might be changed. Through the rabbinical courts and collaboration with the exilarch's regime that set them up, the most effective influence might be attained. Indeed, when we seek to locate the points of contact between the rabbi and the town, we find those points less in the marketplace, synagogue, or in the streets (though the rabbis did not avert their eyes from what happened there) than in the law courts, which were places not only of litigation, but also of administration of all manner of affairs. To direct those courts represented the most convenient and efficient way of doing what the rabbinate wanted. But it must be emphasized again that what the rabbinate wanted was not to *control* others, who would permanently remain essentially outside its circle, but rather win them to the viewpoint of its own estate, to transform the community into a replica of the academy. The rabbis wanted to bring all Israel closer to their Father in heaven, and his traditions as revealed in the whole Torah provided a very full program on how to do so—and what to do after they had succeeded.

## ii. THE ELITE AND THE MASSES

The ultimate issue for the rabbis was not politics but piety: What must one do to serve God in heaven? Piety was manifested by right action in society—and right knowledge of what right action consisted of—and attained by continual study and reflection upon Revelation, which differentiated right from wrong, and by acts of devotion. If the rabbi was the object of divine or angelic favor, that was authenticated not by the miracles he supposedly could perform (though these clearly mattered to everyone) but, in the end, by the rightness of the ideals he advanced in Jewish society. The conviction of Rav Judah is representative:

Rav Judah said, "He who would like to be a man of piety (*hasida*) should carry out the matters of *torts* (*neziqin*) ."

That is to say, the real issues of faith are truly settled in the civil courts and by law. An examination of the rabbis' definition of piety reveals much that would have been comprehensible outside of the academies:

R. Naḥman said, "May I be rewarded for observing three meals on the Sabbath."

Rav Judah said, "May I be rewarded for observing devotion in prayers."

R. Huna b. R. Joshua said, "May I be rewarded for never walking four cubits bareheaded."

R. Sheshet said, "May I be rewarded for observing the commandment of phylacteries."

R. Naḥman said, "May I be rewarded for fulfilling the commandment of fringes."

(b. Shab. 118b)

Such was admittedly the *rabbis'* viewpoint. Unfortunately, in studying the history of Babylonian Judaism, only that viewpoint can be ascertained. Doubtless ordinary Jews would have differed greatly, for their concerns would quite naturally have centered upon the private anguish of common people in any generation: how to sustain life; provide for children; die an easy, dignified death; and achieve salvation, "immortality," or a "portion in the world to come," or in some other way to triumph over personal extinction. But paradoxically it was this most private and personal concern which opened the heart of the ordinary man to the message of the rabbis, for they claimed they knew how to attain that last, least accessible hope through Torah.

That fact is significant, for it underlines a broader conclusion: the people and rabbis were bound together by a common faith. The rabbis may not have approved all that happened in the synagogues, but they did pray with the people. They may not have thought everyone properly used, or understood the meaning of, various holy objects, but they did revere those objects. Their effort was to encase in a shield of laws each and every religious rite, whether people kept the laws or not, and to demonstrate the scriptural foundation for most of what they decreed. Because of their common faith based on Scriptures, the people naturally kept some laws, such as the Sabbath, sexual and dietary taboos, and the like. However, the rabbis thought that these rites ought to be observed in a very particular way. Concerning some kinds of law, the people came to the rabbis with questions, and so were subjected to their influence. For example, women did consult the rabbis about the ritual status of various vaginal secretions. For a very different reason, butchers were subjected to rabbinical control, for the rabbis supervised the markets and had unlimited authority over the slaughter and sale of meat. But the rabbinical prohibition against eating milk with meat was another matter. Many stories exist today about how the rabbis decided what meat was fit and what was not, but there are none about rabbinical supervision over domestic preparation of foods (outside of their own homes). The obvious difference is that in the latter circumstance the rabbis could do no more than pronounce the law and urge people to keep it. They had no basis in Jewish politics to intervene further. So the people and the rabbis believed pretty much the same things; but the rabbis tried to control—they would have said to elevate— and to legislate about objects, rites, and observances either intrinsic to the common faith, or imposed upon it by time, tradition, or customary exegesis.

The Scriptures that brought the elite and the masses together also served to distinguish them from each other. First, although the rabbis were listened to because of their supposedly superior knowledge of the Bible, it was also in their understanding of the meaning of Scriptures that they differed from the masses. The rabbis held traditions which they believed were revealed at the same time as the written text, and these were preserved only in their academies. Hence their effort to find biblical foundations for rabbinical decrees reflected the prior conviction that such foundations had been truly present at the beginning and demanded only to be uncovered. The people, untutored in the ancient traditions of rabbinic schools, obviously understood things differently. What they read in the Bible they obeyed as best they could, for they were normally law-abiding. The rabbis were believed to know what they were talking about, and their supernatural talents encouraged that belief. But the rabbis found much in Scripture which the people did not see, and given the complex and scholastic exegetical devices they used and their rich law traditions, they might well have demanded observances different from what the people could have regarded as truly "Mosaic." If the rabbis had the power—as they did in the matter of the community boundaries for the Sabbath—they did not have to wait to be consulted. For the rest, scriptural eisegesis was the rabbis' chief means of convincing the masses.

A second major difference between elite and masses lay in the rabbis' belief in the overriding value of study of the Torah. In each succeeding generation, they claimed ever more sanctity for the act of study.

R. Huna said . . . "All the exiles will be gathered in only through the merit of the study of the Mishnah [the code of the Oral Torah]. What is the proof-text? *Yea if they engage in oral learning among the nations, I will now gather them up* (Hosea 8:10) ."

He also said, *"For from the rising of the sun even unto the setting of the sun, my name is great among the nations; and in every place offerings are presented to my name, even pure oblations"* (Mal. 1:11) . Now are there pure oblations and the taking off of a handful (of flour) and the letting (of offerings to) go up in smoke in Babylonia? What then is here referred to? It is the Mishnah. The Holy One, blessed be he, said, 'Seeing that you are engaged in the study of the Mishnah, it is as if you were offering up sacrifices.' "

(Lev. Rabbah 7:3)

Obviously the rabbis thought study of the Mishnah a supreme act of piety.

But how would the masses have responded to that belief? They did not study the Torah as did rabbis, and yet they obviously yearned for the ingathering of the exiles and for the arrival of the

Messianic time. They thought that the Scriptures adequately instructed them on what sins to avoid and what virtues to cultivate toward that end. They must therefore have differed from the rabbis at the very crux of the latter's faith: the importance of study of Torah. Other things would have mattered more to them than study of the Mishnah, which, had they been more familiar with the academies, they would have regarded as a training for lawyers and judges only. Lawyers and judges saw their law-studies in a very different light. Study was a supernatural force. Through it, they believed, the natural order of the cosmos would be sustained, empires would be brought low, and the course of history reshaped to Israel's advantage.

Such a fantastic ideal, possible only among the literate, and congruent only to the lives of those able to spend their time in school, could not have meant much to ordinary people. Nor could the rabbis' belief that study was equivalent to Temple sacrifice have pleased either the priests within Jewry or others who thought that the Messiah's coming, which would be marked by the restoration of Temple cultus, must require something more than mere recitation and fulfillment of holy texts. Indeed, if the act of study really meant as much to God as the act of sacrifice which he had formerly required, then why look forward at all to the restoration of the Temple? For ordinary people, both the shape of rabbinic piety and the claim offered in behalf of the intellectual enterprise of the rabbis must have seemed grotesque, an improper and highly inflated evaluation of what was, in the end, of merely social utility and political consequence.

Had the rabbis constituted only a class of literate administrators believed to be endowed with magical powers, but not at all sharing the beliefs of the masses, then one could suppose that the ideal of study would in time have driven a wide breach between the illuminati and the common people. Controlling only the politics of Jewish Babylonia, the rabbis would have achieved limited influence over its piety. The fact is that the rabbis never separated themselves from ordinary Jews so that their ideals became too remote or too difficult. On the contrary, they sought out the ordinary people, looking upon politics as a means to *transmute* their lives, not merely to control them.

The significance in various rabbinical sayings about piety (such as those quoted on page 131, is that the fundamental attitudes expressed in them were by no means appropriate only for a class of illuminati. Rav Judah stressed that piety was a matter of right conduct with one's fellowman, as expressed through keeping the laws of torts and damages, and thus avoiding offense against one's fellow's property or person. The rabbis viewed various ritual commandments —eating to satisfaction on the Sabbath, wearing the proper garments and amulets, etc.—as warranting special reward. None of these rites was applicable only to the rabbinical estate, although during the time under study, it may have been only the rabbinate which kept some of them.

Again it must be stressed that what the rabbi asked of himself, he asked of everyone else. He did not conceive of himself as belonging to a monastic or quasi-priestly caste. He did not set aside special ideals for himself, nor did he place himself above the people by imposing upon himself special rites. Although he may have been high-handed, he was not self-righteous; the rabbi who said, "For my own soul have I studied" was condemned. All Jews were supposed to fear God. All wore phylacteries, fringes, and the like. All were supposed to avoid hurting their fellowmen. And if study was the special activity of rabbis alone, it was not by their choice. Their doctrines were not intended to be esoteric, and their teachings were not meant to be restricted to the elect. Their schools were not closed to all except the especially initiated. On the contrary, though their piety may have differed from that of the masses, their hope was that the time would come, as it did later on, when all Jews would serve God and study the Torah as they now did.

### iii. ONE TORAH FOR ALL ISRAEL

The rabbis present a considerable contrast to the ascetics who lived by ideals not expected of ordinary Christians in the beginning. More striking still is the contrast between rabbinic social policy and that of the dualistic Manichaeans, whom the Zoroastrian Magi thought indistinguishable from the Christians. Even more "monkish" than the Christians, the Manichaeans divided adherents into two groups, each subjected to its own discipline: the elect and the hearers. The two observed entirely different ways of life. The elect were expected to observe complete vegetarianism, to drink fruit juices and not water, to avoid harm to plant and animal life, and to eschew marriage. They dedicated themselves solely to a life directed toward the redemption of their souls; they worked for the reunification of the light particles with the world of light. The hearers, on the other hand, had to undertake all those acts forbidden to the elect but which were in fact unavoidable for the maintenance of life. Thus it fell to the lot of the hearers to furnish the elect with all essential nourishment (Geo Widengren, *Mani and Manichaeism*, trans. Charles Kessler, [London: Weidenfeld and Nicholson, 1965], pp. 95-99). The elect wore wide robes and head-coverings, and the hearers, everyday dress. In short, the Manichaean hearers lived a normal, ordinary life, and the elect did not.

Given the hierarchial organization of Sasanian society, one could hardly be surprised had there been an equivalently stratified structure in the minority communities. Instead, however, the rabbis were eager to diminish in every way the distinctions that set them apart from common folk, by changing—they would have said "raising"— popular patterns of behavior to conform to rabbinical ones. The reason may have been superficially a theological one: all Israel stood at Sinai and equally assumed the obligations of revealed law. But given the exegetical ingenuity of the academicians, one cannot doubt that theological explanations could have been devised for a dualistic social policy, had the rabbis wanted such a policy. The fact is that they did not. They did not see the rabbinate as a separate class of the elect, like the Manichaeans, but rather as the bearer of laws and doctrines which would render all the Jews equally elect. They did not expect the masses to provide the wherewithal for their religious life. One achieved merit by studying the Torah. If the center of piety lay in that study, then all could equally be expected to participate, each according to his abilities. Some would travel wide, others memorize, others merely repeat what they had heard, but all could find a suitable place within the religious enterprise. By contrast, if piety truly required uncommon ascetic disciplines, then only a spiritual elite, ready and able to assume those disciplines, could be asked to become pious or righteous. All others would be "hearers," or outsiders, in the very nature of things. So, paradoxically, the ideal of study which distinguished the rabbinical estate from the masses also drew the rabbis close to the ordinary people and set Judaic social ethics apart from that of other religious communities in Babylonia.

iv. The Rabbinate as a Historical Force

Four primary forces shaped the life of Babylonian Jewry. First was the Sasanian government, which had power to do exactly as it liked with various groups in the empire, and proved it by the way it solved the Manichaean problem. The Manichaeans had posed a severe threat to the Mazdean faith, for they appealed to the same groups upon which the Mazdean church was based—the Iranian component in the population of the western part of the empire. Seen by the Mazdeans as dangerous heretics, they could not be tolerated, but had to be expelled; they were driven out or extirpated as soon as the Mazdean authorities were able to arrange it. The fate of the Manichaeans illustrates what *could* have been done to the Jews, had the Sasanian government so desired. But no reason to expel the Jews existed. The government was perfectly satisfied to oversee Jewish affairs through a loyal agent, to collect their taxes, and to leave them pretty much to their own devices.

It was through the exilarchate that the Sasanians proposed to attend to Jewish affairs, and it thus constituted the second major force in Babylonian Jewish history. As discussed in Chapter Two, the exilarch's duty was to govern the Jews and to carry out among them the policies of the Sasanian regime. Having agreed to do so, the exilarch was given a free hand. In his view, his authority was based upon his distinguished ancestry and upon the support quite naturally accorded to him by the Sasanian government. Even more than the Sasanians, he wanted only to keep the peace and maintain a stable and constructive control of Jewish affairs. The scion of David could ask no less of himself, or promise more to the people, than good government. To govern the people, he sought to apply to their affairs the one law that both they and he recognized as divinely ordained: the Mosaic revelation.

In fulfilling his function, the exilarch increasingly drew upon the personnel and leadership of the third force, the rabbinate. The exilarch made use of these highly motivated lawyers in his administration, although they could not have constituted the whole of it. As the years passed, however, the exilarch faced a new problem. He found that the lawyers and judges, administrators, and teachers educated in the academies were not of one mind about their service to his government. A few of them openly defied his authority, and many apparently regarded his rule as founded upon inferior right. If it was the Torah that was to shape the life of Babylonian Jewry, then its rabbinical masters—who alone were privy to the true meaning of Scriptures—should have the supreme rule, and ought not to remain subservient to one who was supposedly their inferior in knowledge of Torah. Whether the exilarch actually did know less about the Torah than they is no issue here. The fact is that they claimed he did, and even preserved in their records numerous stories of how he had humbly studied the law with his own rabbinical employees.

The fourth force was formed by the largest, but least effective group, the ordinary Jews. There exists today almost no direct knowledge of what they thought about their government and its agents. It has been supposed that they had traditions they believed to be both ancient and correct, and that these would not have conformed in significant ways to the views of the rabbis. But what was more important, they surely must have responded to the presence of a relatively new group or class of religious authorities in their midst in more varied ways than can now be discerned. It is not likely that the ordinary people constituted a party or a group at all. The focuses of their lives were the fields and marketplaces, the homes, streets, and the synagogue. Whatever leadership they had did not extend beyond the given town or village. They were not a "movement" transcending local lines. Where they lived, there alone did they act. They were, so far as can be seen, inert, a great mass to be twisted this way and that, but incapable of guiding or shaping its own growth except in response to events or powers more determined, better organized, and more dynamic than itself. The inertial force of tradition and culture rather than a particular theology or purpose shaped the life of the masses. But one can only guess what that tradition consisted of, beyond Scriptures.

Of the middle groups—exilarchate and rabbinate—the former was a relatively small and self-contained administration, centered upon the person of the Davidic scion and his police and administrators, and based upon the authorization and active support of the imperial regime. The latter estate, which was neither centered upon a single man nor dependent upon the recognition of the government, constituted a party based on schools. Through active proselytizing in the academies and courts alike the rabbinate attracted the support of growing numbers of Jews. Once they accepted the rabbinical claim, those supporters did the things required to effect it: they went, or sent their children, to the academies; they paid proper respect to the great men of the party; they supported its cause by observing its bans and honoring its decrees.

As a party, the rabbinate was a force distinct from the inchoate masses upon which it worked, or the subordinated exilarchate, or the imperial government. The ordinary Jews were not similarly coherent, the imperial government not so purposefully engaged or single-minded, the exilarch not equivalently motivated. Sporadic persecution would not destroy them, nor was such persecution undertaken to begin with. Occasional setbacks would not deter them. While the government ignored them, and the exilarch made use of some, perhaps many, of them for his own purposes, the rabbinate continued to seek every possible means to win over whomever it could to its particular viewpoint on politics and theology and to educate in its schools (and through the exemplars it sent out from them) as many people as possible. So the established forces, the government and its Jewish administration, proved unequal to the task of opposing a well-disciplined, coherent, and certainly well-organized party which in time—though not in the period under study—subverted the latter and thus rendered the former's choices for the Jews quite irrelevant.

From third-century Babylonia onward, "Rabbinic Judaism" was normative; its laws *were* Jewish law; its theology shaped the conceptions of the masses and required the speculative defense of the philosophers; its enemies were designated heretics, and its devotees, the "normative" and "authoritative" exemplifications of Judaism. The rabbinate represents a singularly successful party. In the history of mankind, one can find few "parties" which achieved so lasting a success that, until this very day, their conception of history and society dominates precisely the group which they intended from the beginning to shape and control. There is only one similarly successful group that readily comes to mind, and that is the Christians, who actively undertook to subvert, then control, and finally dominate, the Roman Empire and whose historical role provides an analogy to that of the rabbis. They are not wholly comparable, for the Romans persecuted the Christians sporadically but ferociously, while the patriarchate in Palestine and the exilarchate in Babylonia actually employed the rabbis. The two parties, however, thrived by persistence and faith, and in time succeeded in winning the sovereignty to which they aspired—the one to the Roman world, the other to the rule of Israel. It is only in the past two centuries that either has had to face a significant challenge, a time when the values and ideals of each ceased to shape the groups whom they had dominated for so many centuries.

# Appendix: The Talmud

The Talmud consists of two sections: the Mishnah, a legal code promulgated by Judah the Patriarch in *ca* A.D. 200 in Palestine; and the *Gemara*, or learning, an extensive commentary. The dialectical reasoning of the Talmud was shaped by Roman principles of legal codification and by Greek principles of rhetoric.

Two Talmuds actually exist today, one Palestinian and the other Babylonian. Although both share a common Mishnah, they differ greatly in their respective *Gemara*. Completed *ca* A.D. 500-600, the *Gemara* of the Babylonian Talmud is carefully edited and smoothly constructed according to its own logical sequence of problems and themes. It is formed of several layers of discussion which were produced primarily in the Babylonian rabbinical schools of Sura and Pumbedita. The first layer explains words and phrases and traces authorities for the Mishnaic laws; the second is the result of a more sophisticated search for underlying legal principles, uniting discrete cases; the third is a highly abstract effort to inquire into the foundations of the law and to draw together the results of the first two layers. In general, the rabbis (*Amoraim*) represented in the Babylonian *Gemara* applied to the study of the Mishnah the same acute and sensitive exegetical skills earlier brought to bear upon the study of the Hebrew Scriptures.

The *Gemara* of the Jerusalemite, or Palestinian, Talmud is far less carefully put together. Finished *ca*. A.D. 400-500, it is brief, and its comments are episodic. The dialectical reasoning processes spelled out in the Babylonian Talmud are not brought to full expression. Over the past seventeen centuries, the greatest effort of the Talmudical academies (*yeshivot*) was invested in the Babylonian Talmud, in adding to its commentaries and in codifying its laws.

141

An account of modern scholarship on the problem of the redaction of the Babylonian Talmud will be found in J. Neusner, ed., *The Formation of the Babylonian Talmud. Studies in the Achievements of Late Nineteenth and Twentieth Century Historical and Literary-Critical Research* (Leiden: E. J. Brill, 1970).

A satisfactory translation of the Mishnah is Herbert Danby, *The Mishnah* (London: Oxford University Press, 1933); and of the entire Babylonian Talmud is *The Babylonian Talmud,* translated under the editorship of I. Epstein, 18 volumes (London: Soncino Press, repr. 1948). There is no complete English translation of the Palestinian Talmud.

Introductions to Talmudic literature include Hermann L. Strack, *Introduction to the Talmud and Midrash* (New York: Harper Torchbooks, repr. 1965) and M. Mielziner, *Introduction to the Talmud,* with updated bibliography by Alexander Guttmann (New York: Bloch Publishing Co., repr. 1969).

## THE MISHNAH

The Mishnah is divided into six divisions *(Seder, Sedarim)*, each of which is subdivided into tractates, as follows:

*Zera'im* (Seeds): *Berakhot* (Benedictions); *Pe'ah* (Gleanings); *Demai* (Produce not certainly tithed); *Kila'im* (Diverse Kind); *Terumot* (Heave offerings); *Shevi'it* (Laws of the Seventh Year; *Ma'aserot* (Tithe); *Ma'aser Sheni* (Second Tithe); *Ḥallah* (Dough-offering); *'Orlah* (Fruit of Young Trees); *Bikkurim* (First-fruits);

*Mo'ed* (Feasts): *Shabbat* (Sabbath Laws); *'Eruvin* (Sabbath Limits); *Pesaḥim* (Passover Laws); *Sheqalim* (Sheqel Offerings); *Yoma* (Day of Atonement); *Beṣah* (Festival Days); *Sukkah* (Tabernacles); *Rosh Ha-Shanah* (New Year); *Ta'anit* (Fast Days); *Megillah* (Scroll of Esther); *Mo'ed Qaṭan* (Mid-festival Days); *Ḥagigah* (Festival Offerings);

*Nashim* (Women, family law): *Yevamot* (Levirate Marriages); *Ketuvot* (Marriage Contracts); *Nedarim* (Vows); *Nazir* (Nazirite Vows); *Soṭah* (The Accused Adulteress); *Giṭṭin* (Divorces); *Qiddushin* (Betrothals);

*Neziqin* (Damages, civil and criminal law): *Bava Qamma* (First Gate); *Bava Meṣi'a* (Middle Gate); *Bava Batra* (Last Gate); *Sanhedrin; Makkot* (Stripes); *Shavu'ot* (Oaths); *'Eduyyot* (Testimonies); *'Avodah Zara* (Idolatry); *Avot* (The Fathers' Sayings); *Horayot* (Instructions);

*Qodashim* (Sanctities, cultic laws): *Zevaḥim* (Animal Sacrifices); *Menaḥot* (Meal-offerings); *Ḥullin* (Animals killed for food; secular, not cultic, slaughter); *Bekhorot* (Firstlings); *'Arakhin* (Temple Vows of Valuation); *Temurah* (The Substituted Offering); *Keritot* (Extirpation); *Me'ilah* (Sacrilege); *Tamid* (Daily Whole-offering); *Middot* (Temple Measurements; *Kinnim* (Bird Offerings);

*Ṭoharot* (Ritual Purity Laws): *Kelim* (Vessels); *Ohalot* (Tents);

*Nega'im* (Leprosy signs); *Parah* (Red Heifer sacrifice); *Toharot* (Purities); *Miqva'ot* (Ritual immersion pools); *Niddah* (Menstrual purity laws); *Makhshirin* (Predisposers to uncleanness); *Zavim* (They who suffer a flux), *Tevul Yom* (He who immersed himself that day); *Yadaim* (Hands); *'Uqsin* (Stalks).

Gemara is not available for every Mishnaic tractate. Most tractates in *Mo'ed, Nashim, Neziqin,* and *Qodashim,* as well as *Berakhot* in *Zera'im,* and *Niddah* in *Toharot,* have Babylonian *Gemara;* as for the Palestinian Talmud, its traditions are particularly rich on all of *Zera'im,* but apart from *Niddah,* it has nothing for *Qodashim* and *Toharot.*

In addition, there is a Supplementary Collection—*Tosefta*—for the Mishnah, which contains traditions from authorities (*Tannaim*) who flourished from A.D. 70 to 200 but which were not included in the Mishnah.

## GEMARA

An example of the nature of the Babylonian Talmud's *Gemara* is drawn from the first page of the Babylonian Talmud, Berakhot 2a. The Mishnah is as follows:

From what time may one recite the *Shema'* ["Hear O Israel, the Lord our God the Lord is One"] in the evening?

The *Gemara* is as follows:

On what does the *Tanna* base himself that he commences *from what time?* Furthermore, why does he deal first with the the evening [*Shema'*]? Let him begin with the morning [*Shema'*]!

The *Tanna* bases himself on the Scripture, where it is written, *"And thou shalt recite them [the Shema'] . . . when thou liest down and when thou risest up . . ."* (Deut. 6:7). And if you like, I can answer: "He learns [the precedence of the evening] from the account of the creation of the world, where it is written, *"And there was evening and there was morning, one day"* (Gen. 1:5).

Thus the anonymous commentary explains the authority for, and the editorial principle of, the law on reciting the *Shema'.* The translation (Maurice Simon, trans., *Berakoth* [London: Soncino Press, 1948]) necessarily uses more words in English than are found in the highly succinct Aramaic of the *Gemara.*

A useful selection of Talmudic traditions is C. G. Montefiore and H. Loewe, *A Rabbinic Anthology* (Philadelphia: Jewish Publication Society of America, 1963).

# Suggestions for Further Reading

This book summarizes some of the findings of the writer's *History of the Jews in Babylonia:*
  I. *The Parthian Period* (Leiden: E. J. Brill, 1970²)
  II. *The Early Sasanian Period* (Leiden: E. J. Brill, 1966)
  III. *From Shapur I to Shapur II* (Leiden: E. J. Brill, 1968)
  IV. *The Age of Shapur II* (Leiden: E. J. Brill, 1969)
  V. *Later Sasanian Times* (Leiden: E. J. Brill, 1970)
His other studies on Talmudic Judaism are as follows: *From Politics to Piety: The Rise of Pharisaic Judaism* (Englewood Cliffs, N.J.: Prentice-Hall, 1972) ; *A Life of Yohanan ben Zakkai* (Leiden: E. J. Brill, 1970²) ; *Development of a Legend: Studies on the Traditions Concerning Yohanan ben Zakkai* (E. J. Brill, 1970) ; *The Rabbinic Traditions about the Pharisees before 70,* three vols. (E. J. Brill, 1972; *Formation of the Babylonian Talmud* (cited above) ; *Aphrahat and Judaism: The Christian-Jewish Argument in Fourth-Century Iran* (E. J. Brill, 1971) ; *History and Torah: Essays on Jewish Learning* (New York: Schocken Books, 1965) ; and *Fellowship in Judaism: The First Century and Today* (London: Vallentine, Mitchell, 1963). On the classical Judaic tradition and its encounter with the secular age, this writer's *The Way of Torah: An Introduction to Judaism* (Belmont, Calif.: Dickenson Publishing Co., 1970, in *The Religious Life of Man* series, ed. by Fred J. Streng), and *American Judaism: Adventure in Modernity* (Englewood Cliffs, N.J.: Prentice-Hall, 1971) may also be of interest.

Important essays on Talmudic Judaism are Judah Goldin, "The Talmudic Period," in Louis Finkelstein, ed., *The Jews: Their History, Culture, and Religion* (Philadelphia: Jewish Publication Society of America, 1960), and Gerson D. Cohen, "The Talmudic Age," in Leo Schwarz, ed., *Great*

*Ages and Ideas of the Jewish People* (New York: Random House, 1956).
Talmudic theology is described by George Foot Moore, *Judaism in the
First Centuries of the Christian Era*, three vols. (Cambridge: Harvard
University Press, 1954), and Solomon Schechter, *Some Aspects of Rabbinic
Theology* (New York: Behrman House, 1936).

Salo W. Baron, *Social and Religious History of the Jews* (New York:
Columbia University Press, 1952), vol. II, and Haim H. Ben-Sasson, ed.,
*Social Life and Social Values of the Jewish People,* vol. XI of *Journal of
World History* (New York: UNESCO, 1968), contain useful materials on
the social history of Talmudic Judaism.

Other works on Talmudic Judaism include the following: Leo Baeck,
*The Pharisees* (New York: Schocken Books, 1947); Louis Finkelstein,
*Akiba, Scholar, Saint, and Martyr* (Philadelphia: Jewish Publication
Society of America, 1962), and *The Pharisees* (Jewish Publication Society
of America, 1962[3]); Louis Ginzberg, *Legends of the Jews,* seven vols.
(Jewish Publication Society of America, 1962); Judah Goldin, *The Living
Talmud: The Wisdom of the Fathers* (New York: Mentor, 1957); Erwin R.
Goodenough, *Jewish Symbols in the Greco-Roman Period,* 13 vols. (New
York: Pantheon Books, 1953-1967); and Max Kadushin, *Worship and
Ethics* (Evanston, Ill.: Northwestern University Press, 1964).

The religious life of traditional Judaism is beautifully described by
Herman Wouk, *This Is My God* (Garden City, N.Y.: Doubleday, 1959).
Rabbinic theology has its modern spokesman in Abraham J. Heschel, *God
in Search of Man: A Philosophy of Judaism* (Philadelphia: Jewish Publication Society of America, 1956). The mystical tradition in Judaism, with
important roots in Talmudic times, is described in Gershom G. Scholem,
*Major Trends in Jewish Mysticism* (New York: Schocken Books, 1961).

# Glossary

ABAYE = Babylonian rabbi, *ca.* A.D. 300-350.

ACHEMENIDS = Persian dynasty, ruled Iranian empire from *ca.* 550 to 330 B.C., overthrew Babylonians and restored Jews to Jerusalem.

ADIABENE = province north of Babylonia.

'AQIBA = Palestinian rabbi, *ca.* A.D. 70-130, responsible for the foundations of the Mishnah.

ASHI = Babylonian rabbi, *ca.* A.D. 400, began to lay foundations of the Babylonian Talmud.

BAR KOKHBA WAR = Palestinian revolt against Roman rule, A.D. 132-135.

BARAITA = a tradition allegedly deriving from Tannaitic times, not included in the Mishnah but preserved in the Babylonian Talmud; means "external," that is, outside the canonical Mishnah.

CATHOLICUS = head of the Christian community, equivalent to exilarch. Resided in capital, Seleucia-Ctesiphon.

DAVIDIDES = descendants of the House of David.

DIASPORA = Dispersion, settlements of Jews outside of Palestine.

DURA-EUROPOS = town on Euphrates, north of Babylonia, destroyed by Iranians in A.D. 256. The synagogue in the town, built near the city wall, was filled up with dirt to reinforce the walls, and the synagogue murals were protected so that they were not damaged in the fall of the city. Excavations, beginning in 1929, uncovered the murals, which portray in Greco-Iranian style various biblical scenes and heroes. See Carl H. Kraeling: *The Synagogue,* with contributions by C. C. Torrey, C. B. Welles, and B. Geiger, in *The Excavations at Dura-Europos. Final Report VIII, Part I*, ed. A. R. Bellinger and others (New Haven: Yale University Press, 1956). For interpretation, see Erwin R. Goodenough, *Jewish Symbols in the Greco-Roman Period,* Vols. IX-XI: *Symbolism in the Dura Synagogue* (New York: Pantheon Books, for the Bollingen Foundation, 1964).

EIGHTEEN BENEDICTIONS = prayer, consisting of nineteen blessings, said three times a day.

EXILARCH = ruler of the Jewish community of Babylonia; head of the Exile.

GEZIRPATI = Iranian gendarmes.

HASMONEANS = leaders of the Palestinian Jewish revolt against the Seleucid Greeks *ca.* 165 B.C. Also called Maccabees.

HILLEL = Palestinian Pharisaic rabbi *ca.* 10 B.C.; said, "What is hateful to yourself, do not do to your neighbor. That is the whole Torah. All the rest is commentary. Now, go forth and learn."

ḤIYYA = Babylonian rabbi, *ca.* A.D. 190; settled in Palestine and held a high position in the administration of Judah the Patriarch.

ISHMAEL = Palestinian rabbi, *ca.* A.D. 120; led party of opposition to 'Aqiba.

KARTIR = chief priest of Zoroastrian church *ca.* A.D. 265-285; persecuted Manichaeans, Jews, Christians, Brahmans, and others.

KASHRUT = Jewish dietary laws and taboos.

KETUVAH (pl. *Ketuvot*) = Jewish marriage-contract, protecting woman's rights in case of divorce by guaranteeing alimony.

MANICHAEISM = religion founded by Mani (*ca.* A.D. 226-273), on belief in dualism of light, darkness; good, evil.

MAR 'UQBA = Exilarch *ca.* A.D. 240-270.

MAZDAISM = worship of Mazdah. Also known as Zoroastrianism, after Zoroaster, the great prophet of ancient Iran.

MEZUZAH = amulet posted on doors, containing scriptural passages.

MISHNAH = Code of Law promulgated by Judah the Patriarch of Palestine in *ca.* A.D. 200. Divided into six Orders: on the laws of agriculture; of festivals; of family life; of civil affairs, torts, and damages; of cult; and of ritual purity.

MIDRASH = exegesis of Scriptures.

MOBADS = Zoroastrian priests.

NAḤMAN = Babylonian rabbi *ca.* A.D. 275, related to exilarch of the day.

148

NATHAN = son of the Babylonian exilarch, lived in Palestine *ca.* A.D. 140-175.

NEHARDEA = town in Babylonia where Samuel lived and taught his circle of disciples.

NEZIQIN = torts, laws of damages and civil litigations.

PARTHIANS = Iranian people from northeast of the Caspian who conquered the Iranian empire to the Euphrates River, ruled from *ca.* 240 B.C. to *ca* A.D. 226. Their dynasty was called Arsacid.

PEROZ = Sasanian emperor, d. A.D. 484. Persecuted Christians and Jews.

PERSIANS = Iranian people from southwestern part of the country. Produced Achemenid dynasty (above) and Sasanian (below).

PHARISEES = Palestinian sect, *ca.* 160 B.C.–A.D. 70, included Hillel and other masters; emphasized ritual purity even outside of the Temple, careful tithing of agricultural products. Successors known as rabbis.

PHYLACTERIES = two small square leather boxes containing slips inscribed with scriptural passages and traditionally worn on the left arm and forehead by Jewish men during morning weekday prayers.

PUMBEDITA = town in Babylonia, site of great academy from *ca.* A.D. 297 to A.D. 350, founded by Rav Judah b. Ezekiel, then headed by Rabbah, R. Joseph, Abaye, Rava.

QEDUSHAH = sanctification: "Holy, holy, holy is the Lord of Hosts," prayer included in the Eighteen Benedictions.

RABBAH = head of Pumbeditan academy, *ca.* A.D. 320.

RABBAN = our rabbi: title of Palestinian patriarch.

RAV = early Babylonian rabbi, studied in Palestine with Judah the Patriarch, then settled in Babylonia. Contemporary of Samuel. Lived *ca.* A.D. 180-250.

RAVA = head of Pumbeditan academy, d. *ca* A.D. 355.

SAMUEL = Babylonian rabbi, first great native-born master of the rabbinic tradition, *ca.* A.D. 200-260.

SASANIANS = dynasty produced by Persians, ruled Iranian empire *ca.* A.D. 260-640.

SEDER 'OLAM ZUTA = "Smaller World History," a chronology of the fifty generations from Adam to Jehoiakim and of the thirty-nine generations of exilarch beginning with Jehoiachin. Purpose was to show that the Babylonian exilarchs were descended from David. Probably redacted in eighth or ninth century.

SELEUCIDS = Hellenistic dynasty founded by Seleucus, a general under Alexander and heir to the part of his empire extending through the present-day Middle Eastern countries of Syria, Iraq, Iran, and eastward. They held Palestine after *ca.* 200 B.C. until the rise of the Maccabees in *ca.* 165 B.C., and the lands east of the Euphrates until the rise of the Parthians and their conquest of the Tigris-Euphrates valley, *ca.* 140 B.C.

SHEKHINAH = indwelling Presence of God.

SHEMA‘ = "Hear," name for prayer proclaiming unity of God. "Hear O Israel the Lord our God the Lord is One." Recited morning and night, along with blessings of God as creator of world, revealer of Torah, redeemer of Israel.

SHEQEL = coin.

SHERIRA = Babylonian rabbi, *ca.* A.D. 900; wrote a "letter" explaining history of Talmudic literature and the Talmudic academies.

SUKKAH = booth, built as a temporary shelter for the observance of the festival of Sukkot.

TALMUD = Mishnah plus discussions and amplifications of Mishnah. Two Talmuds exist: Palestinian, completed *ca.* 5th century A.D., and Babylonian, completed *ca.* 7th century A.D. The former contains the Mishnah and the discussions of the Palestinian rabbinical academies; the latter, the Mishnah and the Babylonian ones.

TANAKH = *Torah* (pentateuch), *Nevi‘im* (prophets), *Ketuvim* (writings), tripartite division of Hebrew Scriptures.

TANNA = professional memorizer of Mishnah and Mishnaic traditions. The Mishnah was published *ca.* A.D. 200, not in writing but by oral formulation and oral transmission, and was memorized by the students of the several generations until it was finally written down as part of the Talmud. The *Tanna* of the school was responsible for the official version of the Mishnah. *Tanna* means "repeater," for memorization was accomplished by repeating the tradition orally until it was fixed in memory.

TANNAITIC = pertaining to the period from A.D. 70, destruction of the Temple, to *ca.* A.D. 200, publication of the Mishnah. The rabbinical sages of that period are referred to as *Tannaim.*

WAR OF 66-73 = Palestinian revolt against Rome, resulted in the destruction of the Temple in Jerusalem in A.D. 70.

ZUZ = small coin.

# Index of
# Biblical and Talmudic
# Passages

i. BIBLE

Genesis
1:5 .........143
49:10 ........57
Exodus
22:1 .........35
Leviticus
4:23 .........57
Deuteronomy
6:7 .........143
12:2 .........76
15:11 ........39
28:65 ....... 112
33:3 .........64
II Kings
23:6 .........76
I Chronicles
12:18 ........55
29:11 ........35
Ezra
7:24 .........64
Job
38:15 .......110
Psalms
37:7 .........55
37:11 .......104
39:2 .........55
137 ..........19

Proverbs
8:15 ......55, 58
8:34-36 ......58
Isaiah
59:2 .........83
Jeremiah
28–29 ........42
30:21 .......56
51 ...........42
Ezekiel
23:20 ........35
Hosea
8:10 .....64, 133
Zephaniah
3:15 .........39
Malachi
1:11 ........133
Acts
19:11-20 .....85

ii. BABYLONIAN
TALMUD

'Avodah Zarah
9b ..........70
36a-b .......111
Bava Batra
8a ...........63
164b ........104

Berakhot
2a ..........143
20a ..........83
29a ..........41
29b .........103
58a ..........35
58b .........113
Bava Meṣi'a'
86a ..........78
'Eruvin
45a .........104
54b ..........87
Giṭṭin
7a ...........55
62a ..........54
Horayot
11b ..........57
Ḥullin
127a ........104
132b .......110
Ketuvot
106a .........82
Megillah
7b ..........84
Mo'ed Qaṭan
12b .........75
Nedarim
22 ..........113
62b .........64

Qiddushin
70a-b .........92
71b ..........105
Sanhedrin
7b .........109
47b ..........76
58b .........110
65b ..........84
67b ..........80
98a ..........39
98b .........56
99b ..........103
106b .........82

Shabbat
118 ..........131
139a .........39
Soṭah
21a ..........82
Sukkah
29b .........104
Taʻanit
20b-21a ......107
24a-b ........83
Yevamot
45a ..........75
52a ..........123

iii. PALESTINIAN
     TALMUD

Rosh Hashanah
3:8 ..........39

iv. MIDRASHIM

Leviticus Rabbah
7:3 ..........133
29:1 .........41

# Index
## of Subjects and Names

Abaye
  schools, earth and heaven, 75, 77, 80
  Torah-power, 82-84
Abraham ibn Daud, 68
Academies. *See* Schools
Achemenids, 26, 48, 60
Adda b. Ahva, R., 111
Adiabene, 31, 62, 105
'Agma, 76-77
Aḥai b. R. Joseph, R., 115
Ahasuerus, 82
'Aina' deMayim, 76
Akkadian culture, 28
Alexander the Great, 28
Alexandria, 30, 37
Amasai, 55
Amemar bar Mar Yenuqa, R., 68
Ammi, R., 110
Amos, 120
Amram, R., 104
'Anan, R., 50, 86, 102
Anilai, 31, 104
  Jewish barony, 47-49, 52
Apostles and rabbinic competition, 21, 25
'Aqiba, R., 51, 81
'Aqov, 50
'Aqra, 76

Arbela, 106
Arda, 30, 52
Armenia, 44, 47, 49, 105
Arsacids, 27
Arta, 30
Artabanus III, 31
Artaxerxes, 64-65
Ashi, R., 68, 75
Asinai, 31, 104
  Jewish barony, 47-49, 52

Babai b. Maḥlapta, 73
Babanos bar Qayomta, 72
Babylonian Jewry, 19, 26-29
  Jewish barony, 47-49, 52
  Judaism, 20, 22-23
  Messianic movement, 70
  taxation, 62
Babylonian Talmud, myths, 72
Bahram, 129
Bar Kokhba War, 32, 51, 67, 70, 127
Bel and Beltis, 28
Berik-Yahbeh bar Mame, 72
Beryl, 72
*Book of Tradition*, 68

Canaanites, 87
Capital punishment, 109
Charax Spasinu, 31, 106

Christians, persecutions of, 62-63, 69
Cohen, Gerson, 68
Constantine, 33, 69
Courts, powers over Jews, 116, 119-25
Creative arts, influenced by Torah and Christianity, 24-25
Ctesiphon, 28, 61, 127
    Jewish community, 44-45
Cyrenaica, 30, 37
Cyprus, 30
Cyrus, 26, 60

Dadbeh bar Asmanduch, 72
Danby, Herbert, 142
Darius, 60
Davidic origins, 52-54, 56-61, 66, 71, 101-6, 129, 137-38
Day of Atonement, prayer, 40
Deborah, Song of, 87
Demons, 72-73, 88, 103
Deuteronomy
    taxation of rabbis, 64
    Torah-power, 85
Dinoi bar Ispandarmed, 72
Donag, 91
Dura-Europos, 33, 103, 106

Edessa, 28, 32
Eighteen Benedictions, 40
Elam, 105
Eleazar ben Pedat, R., 55
Eli, House of, 82
Elijah, 35, 102-3
Elisha, 82
Epstein, I., 142
Essenes, 127
Esther, Book of, 82, 121
Exilarchate
    Geniva, political myth, 54-56, 58
    governmental structure, 46-51
    Messianic hope and rabbis, 56-61
    myths and rabbis, 46-51
    rabbinic authority, 101-6,
    rabbinical relations, 45-71, 130
    rabbinical schools, 66-71
    taxation of rabbis, 61-66
    Torah and Messianic hope, 54-61

Exorcism, 72
Ezra, 64, 105

Geniva, 72, 129
    political myth, 54-56, 58
Geyonai bar Mami, 72
Giddal, R., 104
Goths, 50
Grace after meals, 116, 121
Greeks, 28-29
Grosberg, M., *Seder Tannaim ve Amoraim*, 68

Hadrian, 67, 70
Ḥaliẓah, 109, 111, 119
Halwan, 105
Ḥama, R., 76
Ḥama b. Rava, R., 67
Ḥana b. Ḥanilai, R., 113
Ḥananel, R., 50
Ḥanina, R., 69, 80
Hasmoneans, 60
Healing and magic, 72
Helene, Queen, 31
Herod, 30, 60
Hezekiah, 50
Hillel, 57
Ḥinena, R., 50
Ḥisda, R., 110
    Geniva, 55-56
Ḥiyya, R., 51, 54, 57
Hosea, 64-65
Huna, R., 50-51, 91, 133
    bans, 110-12
    community administration, 106-7, 109
    Geniva, 55-56
Huna b. Idi, R., 91
Huna b. R. Joshua, R., 131
Huna b. Mar Zuṭra, 67-68
Huna b. Nathan, 75
Huna Mar b. R. Ashi, 68
Huẓal, 110-11

Incantations, 72-73, 103
Iran
    Babylonian Jewry, 26-27, 42, 45
    taxation of rabbis, 61-66

Isfahan, 69-70
Iṣfahani, Hamza, 69-70
Ishmael, R., 51
Ispandarmed, 72
Izates, 31

Jacob, 56
Jehoiachin, 46
Jeremiah, 89
  co-existence, 41-42
  Messianic hope, 56-57
Jesus, 24-25, 60
Jesus the healer, 72
Joseph, R., 116
  Torah-power, 81-82
Josephus, 30-32, 49, 80, 86
Joshua, 22
Joshua ben Nun, 75
Judah b. Ezekiel, R., 104-5. *See also*
  Rav Judah.
Judah the Patriarch, 42
  armed retinue, 50-51
  Messianic hope, 57, 60
  Mishnah, 53-54, 141
Judaism
  functional power, 98-101
  repressed, 67-71
Julian, Emperor, 44

Kahana, R., 76
Kartir, 33, 129
Komesh, 72

Law enforcement and rabbis, 108-14
*Letter of R. Sherira Gaon,* 67-68
Lewin, B. M., 67-68
Liliths, 72
Loewe, H., 143

Maccabees, 27, 30
Magi, 69-70, 87, 95, 129, 135
Magic, 72-73
  rabbis, 79-81, 88-90
  rabbis and Torah-power, 76-81, 85
Magic bowls, 72-73, 103
Maḥlaphta, 72
Maḥoza, 70, 117
Malachi, 102

Mani, 33, 62
*Mani and Manichaeism* (Geo Wid-
  engren), 136
Manichaeans, 135-37
Marcellinus, Ammianus, 44
Marriage, 105, 122
Martyrdom, 25
Mar 'Uqba, 54-56
Matennah, R., 50
Mazdeans, 129, 137
Mazdewai, 72
Media, 75
Mesene, 105
Mesharshia b. Peqod, 68
Messianic hope
  Babylonian Jewry, 22, 32, 38-41,
    43
  Jewish government, effect on, 67-
    71
  myth and Torah, 54-61
  rabbinic theology, 90
  rabbis and exilarchate, 56-61
  and Torah, 54-61, 79-81
Mielziner, M., 142
Mihr-hormizd bar Mami, 72
Mishnah
  application in Babylonia, 53-54
  explained, 141
  study and piety, 133-34
Mobads, 62, 65
Monobazes II, 31
Montefiore, C. G., 143
Moses, 22, 65
  myths, piety, and "our rabbi,"
    73-74
Moxoene, 105
Myth
  Babylonian Jewry, 22-23
  conflicting myths, 61-66
  exilarchate, 46-51
  rabbis, 51-54
  religious life, 22
  Talmudic contributions, 72
  taxation and rabbis, 61-66
  Torah and Messiah, 54-61, 81-86

Naḥman, R., 91, 129, 131
Naḥman b. R. Ḥisda, R., 63-65

Naḥman b. R. Huna, R., 67-68
Naḥman b. Isaac, R., 63-65
Naḥman b. Jacob, R., 56-57, 59
Naḥum, 50
Nathan of Ṣuṣita, 50-51, 54
Nehardea, 79, 91, 105, 122-23
  Jewish barony, 47-48
Nehawand, 105
Nersh, 117
New Year prayer, 40
Nippur, magic bowls, 72, 103
Nisibis, 48

Ohrmazd, 33
'Oshaia, R., 80

Palmyra, 28, 47
Papa, R., 39, 83, 105
Parthians, Jewish community, 27-32,
  37, 40, 45, 47
Peroz, 67, 69, 71
Pharisaic party, 49
Political myths, 54-56
Poll taxes and rabbis, 61-66
Prayer
  Day of Atonement, 40
  efficacy, 88-90
  Eighteen Benedictions, 40
  New Year prayer, 40
  as power, 40, 43, 131-34
Pumbedita, 76, 79, 91, 104, 141
Purity taboos, 78, 105, 132
Pyl-y Barish, 30, 52

Rabbah, Torah-power, 82-85
Rabbah b. R. Ashi, 67
Rabbah b. Naḥmani, 76-78
Rabbah b. R. Shila, 110
Rabbis
  authority in Jewish society, 101-6
  competition with apostles, 21, 25
  demons, 88, 103
  efficacy of prayer, 88-90
  ethics, 118
  exilarchate, relations with, 44-71,
    130
  health and safety, 107
  historical force, 137-40

Rabbis—cont'd
  holy men, 79-81
  Israel, creating anew, 25
  jurisdiction, 117
  law enforcement, 108-14
  magic, 79-81, 88-90
  magic and Torah-power, 76-81
  Messianic hope and exilarchate,
    56-61
  Moses "our rabbi," 73-74
  myths and exilarchate, 51-54
  piety, 131-34
  political power and religious in-
    fluence, 99-101
  poll taxes, 61-66
  prayer-power, 131-34
  purity taboos, 78, 105, 132
  rain-making, 79
  ritual of "being a rabbi," 90-97
  role of, 129-40
  schools, 66-71
  taxation of, 61-66
  theology, 88-90, 93-97
  Torah: Messianic hope, 54-61;
    power, 99; study, 86-87
Rabina, 97
Rami b. R. Judah, 109
Rav, 50-51, 54-56, 103-5, 113
  bans, 110
  Day of Atonement prayer, 40
  legal reformation, 42
  moral improvement, 39-40
  New Year prayer, 40
  purity laws, 104-5
  schools, 75-76
Rava
  taxation of rabbis, 63-66
  Torah: power, 82-84; schools,
    earth and heaven, 74, 77
Rav Judah, 103
  Geniva, 55
  law enforcement, 110, 112
  piety, 131, 135
  taxation of rabbis, 64
  Torah-power, 82-83
Religious ideas, social changes, 22
Roman Empire and Babylonian
  Jewry, 30, 32, 40

Sabbath, 132-33, 135
  annulment, 67, 69, 71
  court jurisdiction, 121, 123-25
  observances and rabbinic author-
    ity, 104, 106, 115
Safra, R., 57
Sala the Pious, R., 103
Salma, Imma, 72
Samuel, 50, 53, 91-92, 109, 124
  Eighteen Benedictions, 40-41
  law of the land, 33-34, 36, 38-40,
    42
  purity laws, 105
  schools, 76
Saraduŝt b. Shirin, 72
Sasanians
  Babylonian Jewry, 32-38, 40, 45
  taxation of Jews, 62
Schools
  growth to sovereignty, 125-26, 128
  Torah instruction, earth and
    heaven, 73-79
Seder 'Olam Zuta, 49-50
Seder Tannaim ve Amoraim, 68
Sefer HaQabbalah, 68
Seleucia, 28, 47
Seleucia-Ctesiphon, 30-31, 47, 117
Seleucids, 26-30, 37
Shapur I, 33-35, 62, 124
Shapur II, 34, 44, 70
  taxation of rabbis, 62, 65
Shefet, 50
Shehin, 76
Shekheniah, 50
Shemaiah, 50
Sheshet, R., 110, 131
Shila, R., 35-36
Shila of Shelania, R., 75
Shimi b. Ḥiyya, 75
Silk trade, 29, 32, 47
Simon, Maurice, 143
Sin-offering, 57, 66
Small History of the World, 49
Smith, Morton, 80
Social changes from religious ideas,
    22
Song of Deborah, 87
Strack, Hermann L., 142

Sura, 79, 106, 141

Taboos, 78, 105, 132
  court jurisdiction, 121, 123
Talmud
  Babylonian Talmud and Judaism,
    20-21
  explained, 141-43
Taxation, rabbis, 61-66
Temple authority, 48-49
Thackery, H., 86
Tigranocerta, 106
Tigris-Euphrates valley, 26-27, 29
Torah
  creative arts, 24-25
  Israel and one Torah, 135-36
  magic and rabbis, 76-81
  and Messianic hope, 54-61
  Moses, piety and "our rabbi," 73-
    74
  myths and Messianic hope, 54-61
  obedience to, 114-19
  power of Judaism, 98-101
  rabbinic study, 22, 86-87
  ritual of being a rabbi, 90-97
  schools, earth and heaven, 73-79
  symbol of Judaism, 24, 43
  Torah-power, 81-86
Tosfa'ah, R., 68
Trade and commerce, 19, 26, 29, 32,
    45
Trajan, 30, 37, 51
Tyre, 32

'Ulla, 112-13

Vologases I, 47-48
Vologasia, 28, 47

Widengren, Geo, 136

Yalta, 92
Yannai b. Zekhut, 73
Yavneh, 49, 51
  Yohanan ben Zakkai, R., 37-39
Yazdagird, 67-69, 71
Yazdagird II, 69
Yohanan, R., 112-13

Yoḥanan b. 'Aqov, 50
Yoḥanan b. Nappaḥa, 38
Yoḥanan ben Zakkai, R.
  reconstruction, 37-40, 42
  schoolhouse and sovereignty, 126
  sin-offering, 65
  Temple administration, 49

Zamaris (Zimri), 30
Zera, R., 83-84
Zerifa, 76
Zgus, 73
Zoroastrianism, 27, 33-34, 36, 129,
  135